Constructing Mo

Constructing Modern Furniture

Victor J. Taylor

A Drake Publication
Sterling Publishing Co., Inc.   New York

Published in 1980 by
Sterling Publishing Co., Inc.
Two Park Avenue
New York, N.Y. 10016

© Victor J. Taylor
Diagrams by Ken Harvey of Illustrated Arts

ISBN 0-8069-8888-6

First Published in 1977 as Modern Furniture Construction.
Published by arrangement with Evans Brothers, Ltd.
This edition available in the United States, Canada and the
Philippine Islands only

Printed in U.S.A.

Contents

Preface

To many woodworkers the idea that man-made materials could ever be more than a substitute for the real thing would smack of heresy: a proposition not to be entertained by any self-respecting craftsman. Yet one has the suspicion that the great furniture makers of the past would have rejoiced.

For what resources did our predecessors have? Plenty of timber, certainly, and precious little else. Just think—to prepare the simplest piece of wood ready for assembly required labour and sweat that would, justifiably, be called slavery today. That piece of wood had to come from a tree felled by axe and saw, dragged from the forest by horse and team, laboriously erected over the saw pit and even more laboriously sawn into planks. Try to visualize the scene. The 'top man' blinded with sweat, guiding the saw along the mark on a six metre (20ft.) butt, the pit man choked with dust and working in semi-darkness. How accurate could they be in such conditions?

Next came seasoning. They had no moisture metres, just the rule of thumb of one year per 25mm. (1 in.) of thickness and the feel of the timber against the foreman's cheek to tell if it was ready. And then, perhaps, the plank was cleft, or re-sawn, or adzed to bring it down to working sizes.

The jointing of the pieces was a work of art, not necessarily because the workmen wanted it to be but because there were no machine-made screws or nails, and even the best animal glues were temperamental and uncertain in their behaviour. In any case, some joints had to have an in-built allowance to accommodate, say, the movement of a table top against a table rail.

So one can see that the magnificent workmanship of many of the great pieces of the past was not necessarily to prove the abilities of the makers, but rather because it incorporated the only tried and tested methods of over-coming natural disadvantages and shortcomings.

Now we have a wide array of man-made materials before us—plywoods, blockboards, chipboards, synthetic adhesives, upholstering materials. Surely it is time to admit that they are not substitutes but viable materials in their own right which, used with discrimination and knowledge, can produce results our forebears could never have dreamed of?

If this book helps readers to do this, and to make up furniture which will delight them and their families, then it will have achieved its purpose.

Chapter 1
The Timber Situation Today

From time immemorial, trees have been mankind's faithful friend and servant. As a savage, he retreated into the forest for shelter and burned the fallen branches as fuel for warmth. A little later, primitive tools were used to fashion the timber into houses, household goods, tools, and even boats. Certainly there were other materials which he learned to use on his way to civilization—iron, for instance, and clay, and stone. But the one he could work with best, which provided a wide range of necessities, was timber and it was the only one which was self-perpetuating. So from the far-off times of our primitive ancestors to the technology of today, trees and their timber have held a special place in people's hearts.

Until the beginning of the present century the ways of using timber had hardly changed—the tree was felled, sawn into planks and fashioned into what was wanted and if there was a heap of sawdust, shavings, and odd pieces left as rubbish, no one was concerned. There was plenty more where that came from.

However, with the industrial revolutions and population explosions of the nineteenth century things began to change. Industry's appetite for timber was insatiable, and the rising standards of living among the growing populations of the world demanded vast quantities of timber. The First World War brought matters to a head and it was realized, albeit dimly, that the prodigal exploitation of forests could not be allowed to go on.

It was at this time that timber revealed itself as the most adaptable of raw materials. Veneers had been used for centuries (since the time of the ancient Egyptians, in fact), not as an economical way of utilizing timber, but to expose the greatest beauty of the figured grain. With advances in gluing technology, it was realized that veneers could be built up in laminated form to give boards of large size and exceptional stability, and plywood was born.

Another use for this versatile material was discovered, too. Wood could be broken down and pulped to form paper for books and newspaper, and the conifer forests of North America and Scandinavia began to fall beneath the axe.

Between the First and Second World Wars the demand for furniture increased as such things as hire purchase and credit finance enabled more and more people to improve the comfort of their homes. Timbers used for the classical types of furniture such as mahogany and walnut grew scarcer and more expensive and were replaced by oak, beech and birch which were still relatively easy to come by. At the same time, increased mechanization of furniture factories to cope with the demand needed a supply of stable, wide components which would not be affected by changes in humidity and consequently cause hold-ups in production. Plywood obviously met these specifications and was used extensively.

Other man-made boards such as hardboard and blockboard also began to make their appearance. But still at this time there was approximately equal use of solid wood to man-made boards for most furniture. Thus, carcase furniture such as sideboards, wardrobes and chests would consist of a skeletal frame of solid wood infilled (or clad) with man-made boards; all with suitable embellishments and adornments to hide the fact, of course!

The voracious appetite of the Second World War must have swallowed up almost the whole supply of the world's hardwoods then available. Aircraft, buildings, military equipment and furniture all used timber and in addition many thousands of trees were destroyed in the course of battle. It was no wonder that at the end of the war an exhausted world found its timber stocks, particularly of hardwood, had been virtually exhausted.

The situation then, can be summarized in the following way. The 'classical' timbers such as Cuban and Honduras mahogany, and the various walnuts—English, American and European, are very expensive and hard to obtain. The true mahoganies in particular are practically unobtainable. Other hard-to-find timbers (and expensive when you do find them) are: genuine Burma teak, pitch-pine, ebony, and English oak. Most oaks on the market are European, American, or Japanese—all expensive.

Softwoods are readily obtainable but the best grades are quite expensive. Some of the wood on sale today would have been scorned by packing case makers twenty years ago! A South American conifer, Parana pine, is being widely sold and is good value.

One of the most encouraging facts is that quite a large variety of African and Oriental hardwoods can be bought quite easily and relatively inexpensively. They rejoice in exotic-sounding names such as afzelia, gedu nohor, idigbo, jelutong, and most are acceptable as furniture woods.

Such is the timber situation today. In general terms it means that if you want to use solid timber to make a piece of furniture and price is a major consideration your choice is restricted to the following: softwoods of the deal type, reasonably priced and easy to obtain; Parana pine, also easily obtainable and slightly more expensive; tropical hardwoods such as agba, afara, iroko, and ramin which are also fairly readily available from timber merchants but quite expensive; European beeches and oaks, usually from trade suppliers and also expensive. The rarer woods can still be obtained from specialist suppliers but the cost is very high. Let me warn you that if you are looking for timber, either in softwoods or hardwoods, over 200mm. (8in.) or 250mm. (10in.) wide, then your search will be a long and expensive one! Which brings us back to the fact that if you want wide, long components you will have to use man-made boards.

From our point of view, the important changes brought about by the war were the immense advances made in timber technology, gluing techniques, and the beginnings of the plastics industry. We shall be looking at the results of these developments in more detail later, but let it be said here and now that without them the furniture industry, and similar industries using timber products, certainly could not exist in their present form.

Man-made boards

Here are some of the advantages man-made boards have over natural timber.

Boards are manufactured in a range of lengths and widths which are unattainable with natural timber. Thus, one of the most popular sizes is 2440mm. (8ft.) × 1220mm. (4ft.) and it must be obvious that very few trees could even yield a board of this size! Natural timber moves in accordance with changes in the atmosphere around it—in its simplest form, wet weather causes it to swell, dry weather to shrink. Unfortunately, the degree of movement cannot be pre-calculated and allowed for exactly and any accommodation is made by rule of thumb. Cabinet-makers were adept at constructing pieces so that if one part did move, other adjacent parts would not be affected, Chapter 2, Fig. 1. Thus panels were not glued into grooves but left loose so that any movement would be hidden by the grooves and the enclosing framework would not be affected. Table tops, too, were not screwed to their frames but secured by 'buttons' slotted into grooves which allowed a certain amount of movement, (see Chapter 2, Fig. 5).

Man-made boards are, however, quite stable and do not swell or shrink appreciably other than in extreme conditions. Therefore, there is no need for provision to be made to allow for movement although special measures have to be taken in the case of a thin material such as hardboard.

This means that man-made boards need no seasoning period as do natural timbers and this saves a considerable amount of time and the capital which would have to be spent on kilning equipment. On average, a load of timber spends two to three weeks in the kiln, so the saving in time is worthwhile.

Further, man-made boards are consistent in composition and manufacture and, in fact, are required by official standards to conform to detailed specifications. During their manufacture it is possible to incorporate materials or chemicals to impart desired characteristics such as making them waterproof, fire-proof, and rot-proof. It is also very easy to bond a plastic facing of one kind or another to the boards while they are being manufactured. As we shall see, there is a bewildering variety to cover almost any purpose.

Man-made boards score heavily from the point of view of conservation as they utilize almost every part of the tree. Further, many of them are manufactured from softwoods which can be grown as a commercial crop. Hardwoods, which take six or seven times as long to reach usable maturity, cannot be regarded in the same way. Blockboards and battenboards often have cores of such woods as alder or hemlock which are trees not normally used for timber.

However, man-made boards have certain disadvantages; with the exception of plywoods, they are not as strong as natural timber, neither do they have its inbuilt resilience. Those such as blockboards, chipboards, flaxboards and laminboards, cannot be bent to any appreciable extent; this means that furniture built from them must inevitably look 'boxy'.

Moreover, screws and nails do not hold as well in man-made boards as they do in natural timber, but there are special fittings and connectors to overcome this.

Ordinary woodworking tools can be used quite satisfactorily with the boards, but the cutting edges will need sharpening more frequently owing to the blunting effect of the adhesives used in the boards. As there is no grain in man-made boards, it is more effective to use abrading tools like shaper files rather than ordinary bench planes.

If you use a power driven saw to cut man-made boards, it is worth investing in a sawblade with tungsten-carbide tipped teeth as it will give much longer life.

Most man-made boards must have their surfaces covered with some form of facing such as veneer or a plastics laminate, if this has not already been done. Alternatively, the finished piece can be painted. Also any cut edges which show need to be covered or masked in some way, either with veneer or a plastic trim, Fig. 1. Care has to be taken when sawing chipboards and plywoods as the edges of the saw cut can splinter and chip very easily.

Technological advances have had their effect too, on other activities in furniture making, notably improvements in adhesives, plastic polishes which are virtually foolproof, and revolutionary changes in upholstery techniques.

Adhesives

Modern adhesives are a far cry from the old-fashioned glues, though these still have their uses. The traditional Scotch glue was messy to prepare, had to be kept at just the right temperature and was difficult to apply—the parts to be joined had to be warmed before the glue was put on them and then cramped up for hours before the glue set. Nor was the glue waterproof, and

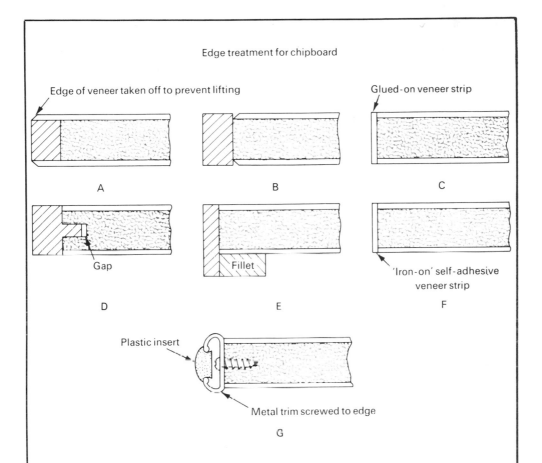

Edge treatment for chipboard

Edge of veneer taken off to prevent lifting

Glued-on veneer strip

A

B

C

Gap

Fillet

'Iron-on' self-adhesive veneer strip

D

E

F

Plastic insert

Metal trim screwed to edge

G

Fig. 1 Edge treatments for chipboard. **A** chipboard panel is edged first with a solid wood beading and veneer is then laid over both the bead and the panel. Such a construction has the inherent danger that the edge of the veneer may lift or 'pick' up, and to combat this the edge of the veneer is bevelled off lightly with a sander. **B** a solid wood bead is used as an edging, but this time the veneer butts against it. Note that the veneer edge is again slightly bevelled off so that if the bead should warp or twist away from the panel the gap will not be so noticeable; **C** the edging consists of a strip of veneer glued on with the grain running vertically; **D** tongued bead edging—the small gap is left to accommodate the adhesive; **E** a neat way to give a thicker and more imposing appearance to the edge by using a solid wood bead plus a fillet glued and pinned on; **F** shows the use of a self-adhesive veneer strip that can be ironed with a domestic iron; **G** a proprietary form of metal trim with a plastic insert.

a period of a few years in a damp environment could cause it to perish and the joint to part.

Today, plastics technology has provided adhesives that are immensely strong and easy to apply, and which can be used either indoors or outside. Further, the setting times vary from immediately on contact to 24 hours or more, depending on the type of work. Bonds that were virtually impossible in the old days are now simplicity itself—glass to glass, for example, or metal to metal.

Finishes

Our debt to industrial chemistry includes the advances made in wood finishes. Modern plastics finishes can simply be brushed on, allowed to set for a few hours, and the result is an iron-hard surface that is resistant to almost everything. They do not have the lustrous depth of French polish, although when applied coat-on-coat they approximate to it very nearly, but they do not mark like French polish which is particularly prone to show water or spirit stains.

Upholstery

Perhaps the greatest revolution has been in upholstery techniques, now that slabs of latex or plastics foam have replaced the laborious networks of such things as webbing, springs, flock, and horsehair.

Personally, I think that the most comfortable springing of all was the old-fashioned kind as it had a firm resilience that foams cannot give. However, I am more than ready to concede that the small loss of comfort is a slight price to pay for the ease and confidence with which we can now take on upholstered work of the most complicated kind.

It may seem that I have been at pains to disparage the old methods and the old materials, but this was not my intention. The point to be made is that for most of us the only materials easily available are those I have been describing.They should not be regarded as substitutes for the real thing, but as woodworking materials in their own right calling for the different methods and techniques with which this book will be concerned.

Chapter 2
Comparing the Old and the New

Carcase framework

Fig. 1 shows a basic framework, variations of which would have been used for such furniture as court cupboards, sideboards, chests of drawers, and

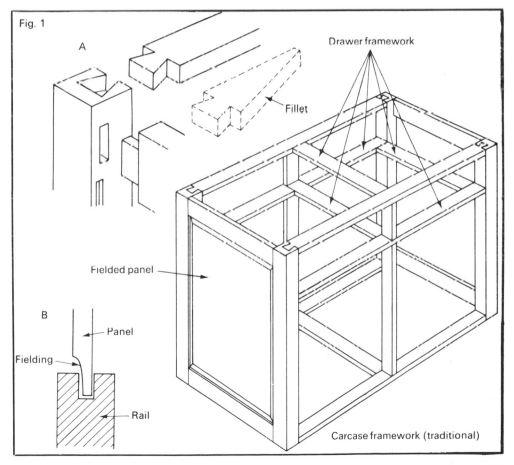

Fig. 1

A

Drawer framework

Fillet

Fielded panel

B

Panel

Fielding

Rail

Carcase framework (traditional)

wardrobes. Note the corner assembly shown at A where the top of the corner post has a dovetail socket cut in it, plus a mortise to accept the tenon on the end rail, plus a groove for the panel. Quite often a triangular fillet (shown dotted) was also embodied, being dowelled to one rail and dovetailed to the other.

The result was, of course, a very strong and robust joint which was capable of resisting all the strains imposed upon it by either physical handling or shrinkage. But think of the work involved! I think you would be lucky to cut and fit two such joints in a day even if machinery were available.

The remainder of the joints would probably be mortise and tenon. At B you can see how the fielded panels are housed into grooves in the rails, no glue being used so that the panels are free to move. If this were not so, they would almost certainly shrink and split. Fielding refers to the tapering-off of the edges of the panels—this means that a comparatively narrow groove can be used to house quite a thick panel without weakening the rail too much. And it does give an elegant finish to any panelling.

Now let us look at its equivalent made up from man-made boards, Fig. 2.

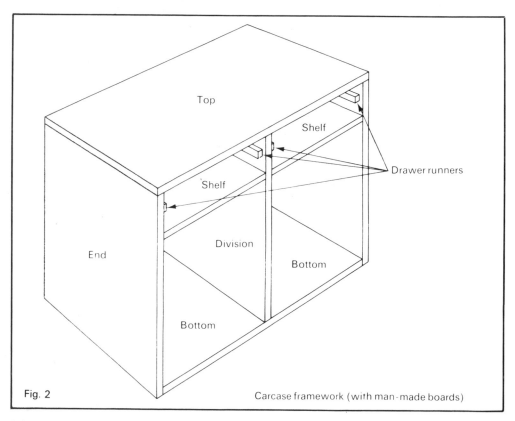

Fig. 2   Carcase framework (with man-made boards)

Frankly, there is not much to say because the construction is so basic and self-evident; in fact, if someone with no knowledge of construction had to design a sideboard, this is probably what he would finish up with!

The several ways of jointing the boards are given in Figs. 3 and 4 together with details of drawer front and side joints. In traditional construction, the drawer fronts and sides were invariably dovetailed together to impart square-ness and rigidity to the drawer. With the negligible risk of shrinkage in man-made board, this is no longer necessary and the joint can be made much simpler.

Table framework

The traditional method is shown in Fig. 5, and as you can see, three of the rails were 'buttoned' to the top to allow for movement while the front rail was pocket-screwed.

Buttons are simply small blocks of scrapwood shaped with a tongue and screwed to the underside of the table top; the button is swivelled so that the tongue engages in a groove cut in the rail. Actually, buttons are usually made wrongly in that the tongues are made rectangular in section; strictly speaking, the tongue should have a slight taper on its thickness so that the further it enters the groove the tighter it wedges itself.

Note, too, the haunched tenons used on the rails; the haunch gives added strength to the joint while the ends of the tenons are mitred at 45 deg. so that they meet in the centre of the leg.

Pocket-screwing is self-explanatory and indeed can be used just as successfully with man-made boards as with traditional materials.

One way of fixing the rails to the leg by means of a steel brace plate is illustrated in Fig. 6. The rails are dowelled and glued to the leg and a dowel screw is inserted into the leg, (see Chapter 11, Fig. 25). You will need to cut a slot into each of the rails to accept the flange of the brace plate, the latter being tightened down on the dowel screw by means of a wing nut.

Pocket-screwing is very suitable for fixing down the top to the rails but there is another way which is by means of jointing blocks. These are made of plastic and details are shown in Chapter 11, Fig. 12; they are capable of many applications and can make a really strong joint.

Small chair frames

The most important joint on a small dining-chair is the one where the side rails meet the back leg as it has to resist enormous racking strain when the

Fig. 3 (above) Dovetail joints in **A** chipboard, **B** multi-ply and **C** blockboard. Of the three materials plywood gives the best results, followed by blockboard, with chipboard rather a long way behind.

Fig. 4 Joints in plywood. **A** rebated joint, fixed with nails and glue. A straightforward joint, but too large a nail size may split the plies as shown; **B** a form of cross-halved joint. The hole, the diameter of which equals the thickness of the panel, is bored first and then saw cuts are made to meet it; **C** a useful guide to screw sizes for various thicknesses of plywood; **D** through dovetail joint, for greatest strength the pins and tails should be approximately equal; **E** a lapped dovetail joint; the same remarks apply to this and to **F**, the secret mitre dovetail joint; **G** a very strong right angle joint made with a series of barefaced tongues fitting into mating blind slots. **H** mitred joint with hardwood tongue. Note that the tongue needs to be slightly nearer to the inside of the joint so that the greatest width can be employed. **I**, **J**, and **K**, are three plan views of plywood drawer fronts.

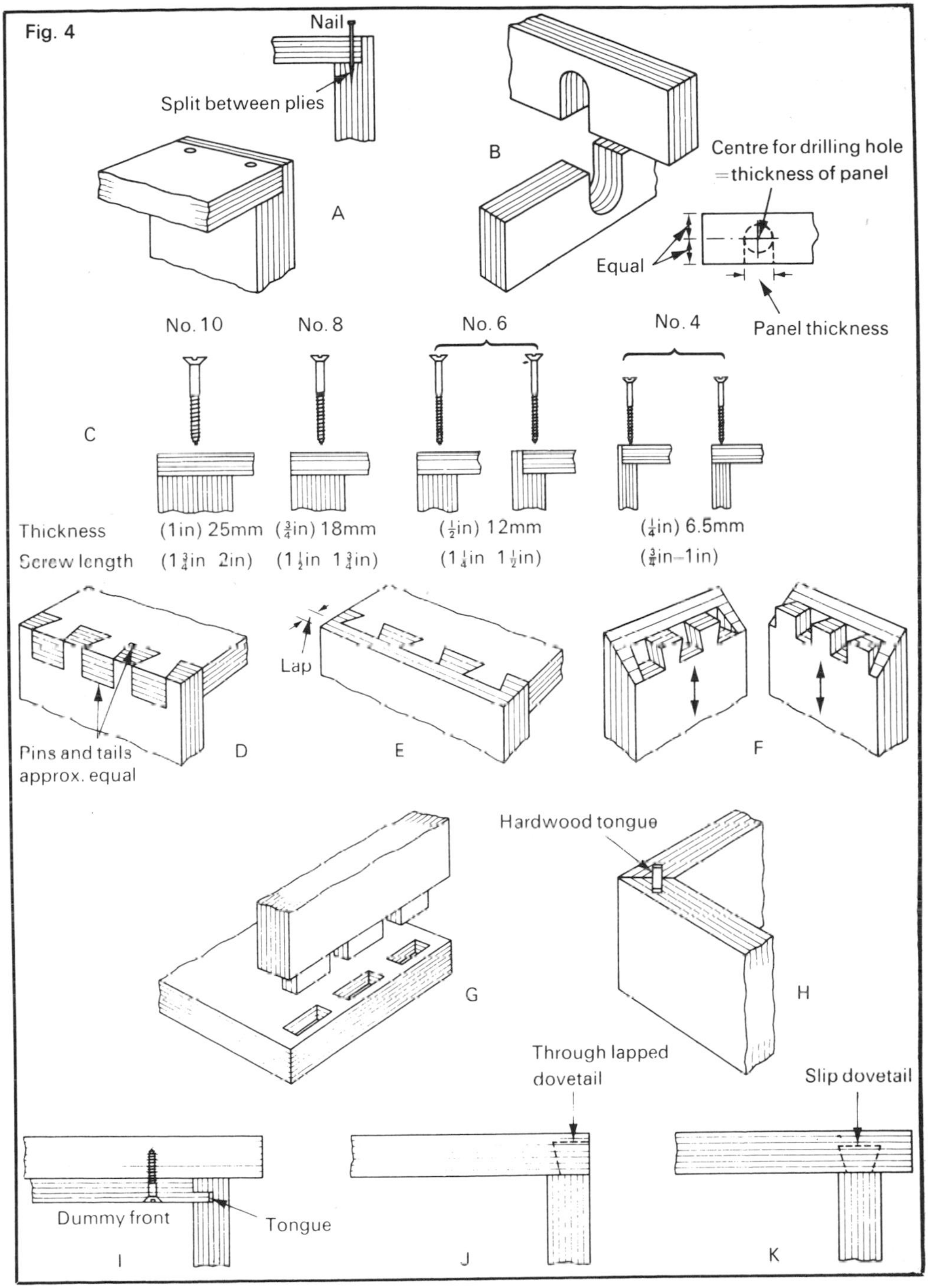

Fig. 4
Nail
Split between plies
A
B
Centre for drilling hole
=thickness of panel
Equal
Panel thickness
No. 10
No. 8
No. 6
No. 4
C
Thickness
(1in) 25mm
(¾in) 18mm
(½in) 12mm
(¼in) 6.5mm
Screw length
(1¾in 2in)
(1½in 1¾in)
(1¼in 1½in)
(¾in–1in)
Lap
Pins and tails
approx. equal
D
E
F
G
Hardwood tongue
H
Through lapped
dovetail
Slip dovetail
Dummy front
Tongue
I
J
K

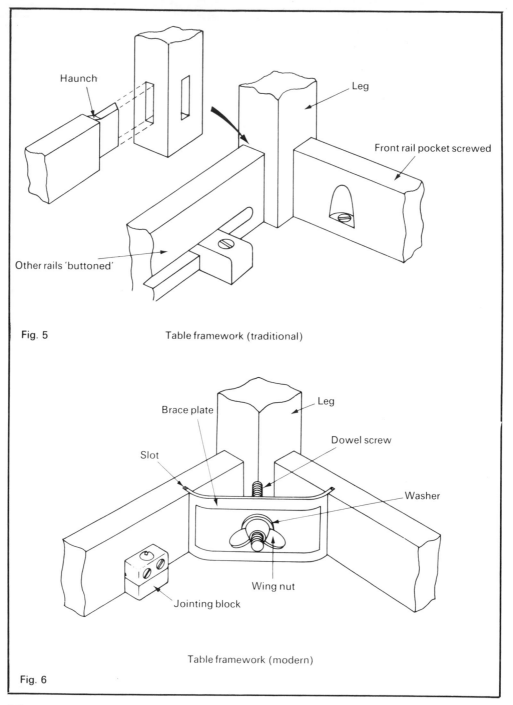

Haunch

Leg

Front rail pocket screwed

Other rails 'buttoned'

Fig. 5   Table framework (traditional)

Brace plate

Leg

Dowel screw

Slot

Washer

Jointing block

Wing nut

Table framework (modern)

Fig. 6

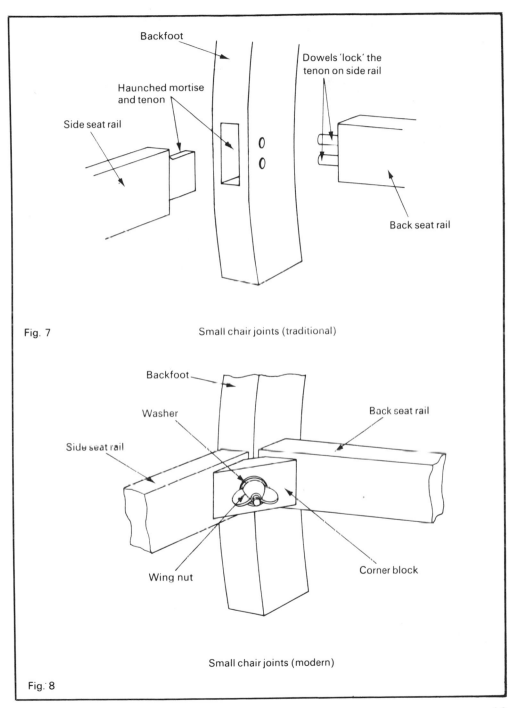

Backfoot

Dowels 'lock' the
tenon on side rail

Haunched mortise
and tenon

Side seat rail

Back seat rail

Fig. 7

Small chair joints (traditional)

Backfoot

Washer

Back seat rail

Side seat rail

Wing nut

Corner block

Small chair joints (modern)

Fig. 8

19

Fig. 8A Typical use of a dowel screw, with wing nut and washer, to strengthen a chair leg joint.

occupant leans back and tips the chair up. Obviously, the joints on the front legs are important, too, but they do not have to withstand this kind of punishment.

As the majority of small chairs still use natural timber for their legs and rails, the traditional joint shown in Fig. 7 is still as relevant as ever it was. It is extremely strong—note that the dowels in the back seat rail are arranged to penetrate the tenon on the side seat rail for maximum rigidity.

However, there is a modern way of doing the same job although in my experience it is not as strong as the traditional joint. The method is shown in Figs. 8 and 8A where a corner bracket is glued between the back and side seat rails. It has a hole bored centrally which accepts a dowel screw. Tightening the wing nut pulls the joint up together, the seat rails are dowelled and glued to the backfoot.

Chapter 11, Fig. 25 also shows details of the dowel screw which, although humble, is capable of as many applications as a K.D. fitting.

Upholstered furniture

This is undoubtedly the area where the greatest changes have taken place. Fig. 9 shows the traditional method of upholstering an easy chair, with the first stuffing completed. The second stuffing entails covering the first with

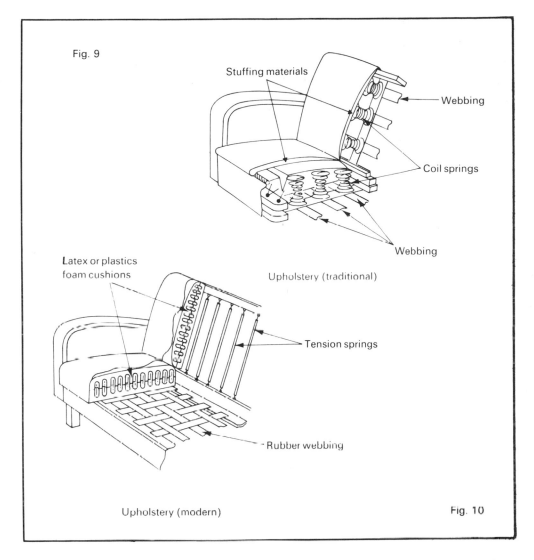

Fig. 9

Stuffing materials

Webbing

Coil springs

Webbing

Upholstery (traditional)

Latex or plastics
foam cushions

Tension springs

Rubber webbing

Upholstery (modern)

Fig. 10

a layer of linters felt (cotton linters) which is stitched in place, and then applying the final covering material. The whole thing is a mass of webbing, springs, and various kinds of stuffing and the upholsterer needed to be highly skilled, as indeed he was.

In Fig. 10 the much simpler present-day method is illustrated. Here, the complicated webbing and springing is replaced by rubber webbing on the seat and tension springs in the back—the latter could equally well be serpentine springing. The seat and back cushions could be either latex foam or plastics foam.

Chapter 3
Blockboards and Particle Boards

Blockboard and laminboard

Both blockboard and laminboard consist of a core of rectangular strips of wood which are aligned edge to edge and then sandwiched between outer plies, see Fig. 1.

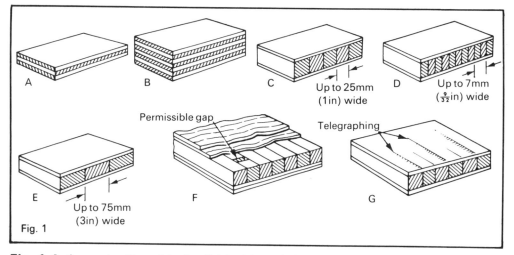

Fig. 1

Fig. 1 A three ply; **B** multi-ply; **C** blockboard; **D** laminboard; **E** battenboard; **F** typical permissible gap between core strips in blockboard; **G** how 'telegraphing' affects the outer veneers.

In the case of blockboard the core strips can be from 8mm. ($\frac{5}{16}$in.) up to 25mm. (1in.) wide and may be assembled with or without adhesive. If there is one outer veneer each side the board is called a 'three ply' one, but other boards can have two outer veneers each side and are called 'five ply'. As a general rule, if the length of the board exceeds the width then it should be five ply. Note that the core strips always run the length of the board, and that there may be small gaps up to 3mm. ($\frac{1}{8}$in.) wide between the strips; this is not detrimental.

Laminboard is a heavier and more expensive type of blockboard in which the core is built up from wood strips or veneers from 1.5mm.–7mm. wide ($\frac{1}{16}$in.–$\frac{5}{16}$in.) glued face to face. It is particularly suitable for high-class work as the fault of 'telegraphing' which can happen with blockboard does not occur. Telegraphing is the name given to the effect whereby the core strips of the blockboard impart a ripple to the appearance of the outer veneers and this, unfortunately, often does not show up until the board has been given a high finish.

Battenboard is a variation of blockboard construction in that the core strips can be wider—up to 75mm. (3in.), in fact.

Gradings

All of these boards are for interior use only unless there is a specific statement to the contrary. Gradings exist for blockboards, as under:

Bonding INT. In this grade, the adhesives used must make strong and durable bonds under dry conditions, although they will tolerate a limited amount of moisture. In addition, they need not be resistant to micro-organisms such as fungi.

Bonding MR. In this group are included adhesives which may last for a few years in full exposure to the weather. They will also withstand cold water (e.g. damp) for a long period and are highly resistant to micro-organisms.

Bonding BR. These adhesives have good resistance to weather but will eventually fail under full exposure. Also highly resistant to micro-organisms and to cold water conditions.

The effect in these gradings is that although they specify the exact requirements of the adhesives, there is no guarantee that the wood itself will measure up to the same standards.

Now that timber has been mentioned, it would be a good idea to look at some of the woods used for the facing veneers and the core strips. The former include agba, beech, birch, gaboon, gedu nohor, limba, African mahogany, obeche, poplar, and seraya. The latter include fir, gaboon, obeche, pine, poplar, spruce, Western red cedar.

The principal sizes are as follows:

5100mm. × 1830mm. (16ft. 9in. × 6ft.)
4575mm. × 1525mm. (15ft. × 5ft.)
4495mm. × 1525mm. (14ft. 9in. × 5ft.)
3660mm. × 1830mm. (12ft. × 6ft.)
3660mm. × 1525mm. (12ft. × 5ft.)
3480mm. × 1830mm. (11ft. 5in. × 6ft.)
3050mm. × 1525mm. (10ft. × 5ft.)

2440mm. × 1525mm. (8ft. × 5ft.)
2440mm. × 1220mm. (8ft. × 4ft.)

Thicknesses are: 13mm. ($\frac{1}{2}$in.); 16mm. ($\frac{5}{8}$in.); 18mm. ($\frac{11}{16}$in.); 19mm. ($\frac{3}{4}$in.); 22mm. ($\frac{7}{8}$in.); 25mm. (1in.); 38mm. (1$\frac{1}{2}$in.); 48mm. (1$\frac{7}{8}$in.).

Particle board

The exact definition of a particle board is one which is made from wood chips alone, or wood chips plus other ligno-cellulosic material, or ligno-cellulosic material alone. Ligno-cellulosic material in this context refers to Bagasse board which is made up from the residue of sugar cane, or flax board which is made from flax shives which are the residue of processing the flax plant. In each case, the particles are bonded with a synthetic resin adhesive and/or other organic binder, and the boards are suitable for interior use only unless there is a definite specification to the contrary.

The boards we shall be dealing with are wood chipboards, composed of wood chips. There are two principal types of these, extruded and platen-pressed.

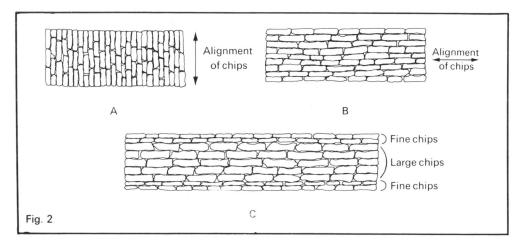

Fig. 2

Fig. 2 A extruded chipboard; **B** platen-pressed chipboard; **C** chipboard with graded chips.

Extruded chipboard. This kind of board, Fig. 2A, is made by forcing the mixture through a die with the result that the particles align themselves in a perpendicular formation at right angles to the board surface. As you would expect, this formation is inherently weak and the boards are not recommended for any kind of structural work but only for infilling and cladding.

Platen-pressed chipboard. Such boards as those at Fig. 2B are made by pressing the chips-plus-adhesive mixture between platens (rollers) so that it emerges to the required thickness. This is the material that the layman is thinking of when he talks about 'chipboard' and it is also the kind of board widely used in woodwork.

Chipboards are graded according to their density into high, medium, and low densities. High density is a minimum of 800.9Kg. per cubic metre (50lb per cubic foot), medium density a minimum of 400.5Kg. per cubic metre (25lb per cubic foot), and low density covers boards less than 400.5Kg. per cubic metre.

From our point of view, however, the general trade custom is to classify boards from the lightest usage upwards, thus: extruded grade (400 density), furniture grade (500 density), furniture/building grade (600 density), building grade or flooring grade (680 density), and heavy-duty building grade (700 and 720 densities).

As we have seen, extruded boards are best used for non-structural, non-loadbearing work such as wall or partition linings, in-filling carcase frames and in particular any jobs where sound absorption is needed.

The use for furniture grades is self-evident; building grades are used for surfaces subjected to heavy wear such as flooring, shop counters, and furniture and fittings in public uses. Heavy-duty grades are utilized for concrete shuttering, roofing and so on.

In addition to the homogeneous kind of board in which all particles are the same material and the density is the same throughout, there is a multi-layer (usually three layer) particle board in which at least two or more layers of particles differ in their size and nature, Fig. 2C.

You will also find that there are boards containing additives which confer a special quality. For instance, small quantities of paraffin wax can be introduced during manufacture to give moisture resistance, while the addition of borax helps fire resistance. Some boards are rot-resistant because of insecticides or fungicides incorporated during manufacture.

Boards can be obtained in a variety of surface finishes. On some, sawdust is sprinkled on the surface in the final stages of manufacture to give a smooth, fine finish while others purposely have large particles embedded near the surface so that the board presents a mottled appearance. Wood veneers are widely used, too, as a facing material and in this case the reverse side of the board should also be veneered to prevent 'bowing'. This veneer is called a 'balancer' and compensates for any pulling force exerted by the surface veneer.

The ubiquitous plastics laminate is employed too, as a facing material, and one can even get boards which are primed ready for painting.

Particle boards are made in a multiplicity of sizes and since a great number are made in Europe, the dimensions are in millimetres. Even so, although metric, the dimensions are equivalent to Imperial feet and inches, so a kind of benevolent compromise presides over everything! If you remember that 305mm. = 12in. approx., and that 25mm. = 1in. approx., you will not find it confusing when you are confronted with metric sizes.

Here are the lengths and widths most readily available:

1220mm. × 2440mm. (4ft. × 8ft.)
1220mm. × 2745mm. (4ft. × 9ft.)
1220mm. × 3050mm. (4ft. × 10ft.)
1220mm. × 3660mm. (4ft. × 12ft.)
1220mm. × 4880mm. (4ft. × 16ft.)
1220mm. × 5185mm. (4ft. × 17ft.)
1525mm. × 2440mm. (5ft. × 8ft.)
1525mm. × 4880mm. (5ft. × 16ft.)
1525mm. × 5185mm. (5ft. × 17ft.)
1725mm. × 2745mm. (5ft. 8in. × 9ft.)
1830mm. × 2440mm. (6ft. × 8ft.)
1830mm. × 3660mm. (6ft. × 12ft.)
2440mm. × 3660mm. (8ft. × 12ft.)

And here are the thicknesses which are most commonly used—there are others but you may have difficulty in obtaining them. (The imperial measurements are the accepted nearest equivalents.) 9mm. ($\frac{3}{8}$in.); 12mm. ($\frac{1}{2}$in.); 15mm. ($\frac{5}{8}$in.); 18mm. ($\frac{3}{4}$in.); 22mm. ($\frac{7}{8}$in.); 25mm. (1in.).

Flaxboard

This can be compared to a medium density chipboard, although it is lighter in weight. It finds large-scale use in furniture as a core for veneered stock and if you can get hold of it, you will discover how good it is for this.

Gradings are by density, as for chipboard, and are: 400, 450, 500, 525, 550, and 600.

Thicknesses are: 8mm. ($\frac{5}{16}$in.); 10mm. ($\frac{3}{8}$in.); 12mm. ($\frac{1}{2}$in.); 15mm. ($\frac{9}{16}$in. full); 16mm. ($\frac{5}{8}$in.); 18mm. ($\frac{11}{16}$in. full); 20mm. ($\frac{3}{4}$in. full); 22mm. ($\frac{7}{8}$in.); 24mm. ($\frac{15}{16}$in. full); 26mm. (1in. full); 30mm. ($1\frac{3}{16}$in.); 34mm. ($1\frac{3}{8}$in. bare); 36mm. ($1\frac{7}{16}$in. bare); 40mm. ($1\frac{9}{16}$in. bare); 44mm. ($1\frac{3}{4}$in.).

Sizes are:

1220mm. × 2440mm. (4ft. × 8ft.)
1250mm. × 2540mm. (4ft. 1in. × 8ft. 4in.)
1710mm. × 3510mm. (5ft. 7in. × 11ft. 6in.)
1725mm. × 3510mm. (5ft. 8in. × 11ft. 6in.)
1725mm. × 4250mm. (5ft. 8in. × 13ft. 11in.)
1810mm. × 4250mm. (5ft. 11in. × 13ft. 11in.)
1830mm. × 4250mm. (6ft. × 13ft. 11in.)
1850mm. × 3510mm. (6ft. 1in. × 11ft. 6in.)

Hardboards

Probably the most versatile and certainly the easiest obtainable of all boards, hardboards have been in existence now for thirty years or more and have certainly proved their worth.

Technically the boards are composed of ligno-cellulosic fibres (softwood pulp) massed together to give uniform strength in all directions, and additives are introduced during manufacture to provide boards with special qualities. One side has a smooth surface while the reverse has a woven mesh pattern; double-sided smooth faced boards are available, however.

Basically there are three types of board—standard, medium, and tempered which are each re-graded and distinguished by coloured stripes on the edges of the board.

Standard boards. These have one blue stripe and have the code letter S.

Medium boards. These are subdivided into four classes, HME, HMN, LME, LMN. The letters HM indicate that the boards are high density, and LM denotes low density. The suffix E means that the quality is the highest manufactured, but N indicates that the board, while perfectly suitable for normal usage, does not meet the more stringent tests associated with grade E. The colour codings are: HME, 2 black stripes; HMN, 1 black stripe; LME, 2 white stripes; LMN, 1 white stripe.

Tempered boards. These are also called 'oil-tempered' or 'super' boards and include additives which make them weather- and water-resistant provided you take certain precautions which will be discussed on page 74. There are two gradings—TE and TN, and again the suffix E denotes that the board satisfies the most stringent requirements. The colour codings are: TE, 2 red stripes; TN, 1 red stripe.

Here are some more kinds of boards which are widely available: plastic-faced hardboards; metal-faced hardboard; enamelled hardboards; wood-veneered hardboards; embossed hardboards; perforated hardboards.

Board sizes in common use are:

762mm. × 1981mm. (2ft. 6in. × 6ft. 6in.)
915mm. × 2135mm. (3ft. × 7ft.)
915mm. × 2440mm. (3ft. × 8ft.)
1220mm. × 1220mm. (4ft. × 4ft.)
1220mm. × 1830mm. (4ft. × 6ft.)
1220mm. × 2440mm. (4ft. × 8ft.)
1220mm. × 2745mm. (4ft. × 9ft.)
1600mm. × 2440mm. (5ft. 3in. × 8ft.)
1700mm. × 2440mm. (5ft. 7in. × 8ft.)

Board thicknesses in common use are: 3.2mm. ($\frac{1}{8}$in.); 4.8mm. ($\frac{3}{16}$in.); 6.4mm. ($\frac{1}{4}$in.); 9.5mm. ($\frac{3}{8}$in.); 12.7mm. ($\frac{1}{2}$in.); 19.1mm. ($\frac{3}{4}$in.); 25.4mm. (1in.).

Chapter 4
Plywoods and Plastics Laminates

Plywood boards are composed of veneers or plies bonded together and pressed under heat to form the familiar sheets.

One of the most important points to watch for when buying plywood is the method by which it was dried and glued. The 'dry cementing' process produces the best results; the other two methods called the 'wet' process and the 'semi-dry' process yield boards which are not of such high quality. They are more likely to warp and twist and also to contain tiny surface splits called 'checks' which may render the boards unsuitable for painting, varnishing, polishing, or veneering.

The veneers are laid at right angles to each other to distribute their longitudinal strength in all directions and to give rigidity and stability. As the grain of the face veneers on the opposite sides of the sheet must run in the same direction to balance out the opposing strains of the individual veneers, it follows that any board must always have an odd number of plies (e.g. 3, 5, 7, 9 and so on) and never an even number.

Plywoods classed as Interior grade, which is the grade used for most furniture, may be bonded from any one of the following three adhesives:

1. Animal glues. Made, for example, from hide or offal. These give an excellent bond under dry conditions but are very susceptible to moisture and to moulds and fungi. However, they are quite suitable for normal domestic environments,

2. Blood albumen glues. These give a moderately strong bond, but in damp conditions can be liable to breakdown through fungal or mould attacks.

3. Casein glues. These consist of a mixture of milk curds, hydrated lime, and other chemicals and the resulting bond is a good, strong one. They must not be exposed to prolonged conditions of damp, however, otherwise fungal or mould attack will destroy them.

Plywoods bonded with synthetic resin adhesives. There are a great many, notably Urea-formaldehyde (UF), Urea-melamine-formaldehyde (UMF), Phenol-formaldehyde (PF), and Resorcinol-formaldehyde (RF).

Moisture-resistant plywoods. These are classed as MR, use UF adhesive and have a very high bonded strength. The bond will withstand prolonged soaking in water at normal temperature and will survive out-of-doors in moderate conditions, but will break down under continuous exposure to extreme weather conditions. Such plywoods are immune to attack by micro-organisms such as fungi.

Boil-resistant plywoods. These are classed as BR, and are so-called because of their resistance to immersion in boiling water, which is one of the standard tests. In dry conditions the bond-strength is the same as MR, but it will survive more severe conditions out-of-doors. As with MR, it is immune to attack by micro-organisms. The adhesive used is UMF.

Weather and Boil-proof plywoods. These are classed as WBP, bonded with PF, and are pre-eminent in exposed and adverse weather conditions, surviving long periods without breakdown. They are also immune to micro-organism attack.

The RF adhesives are too expensive to be used widely in plywood manufacture, except for special purposes. They are, however, used as fortifiers in conjunction with other adhesives, as their resistance to severe exposure is second-to-none.

Extenders

As a matter of interest, you may like to know a little about these materials. These are mixed with the expensive synthetic resin adhesives to make them easier to manipulate and go further, bearing in mind that the general method of spreading the adhesive is by rollers.

Some typical extenders are rye flour, soya flour, and other vegetable flours, while resin and/or blood albumen are also used. I must point out, however, that if you are tempted to adopt the practice in your workshop there is nothing to stop you. But please do get exact data from the adhesive manufacturer as the proportions of extender to adhesive are highly critical.

Surface treatments

There are several different ways of treating the surfaces of plywood. One of the most common is to veneer it with a decorative veneer, in which case the reverse face should be veneered with a 'balancer'—usually a cheaper, plainer veneer.

Another finish needing no further treatment is created by applying a polyester lacquer by means of a curtain-coater, and this is called 'pre-finished' plywood. It is available either as a plain finish, or with light V-grooves cut in the surface to give the impression of planking.

'Printed plywood' is a fairly recent development and involves spraying a coat of the basic colour on the surface. After drying, the board is passed through several printing rollers to produce the desired pattern and colours. As the surface is a dull finish it only needs an occasional rub over with wax polish.

There are also plywoods for special purposes such as concrete form work, ships' bulkheads, or with flame retardant properties, but these are outside our scope.

Classification of plywoods

This is difficult as it appears to be an international free-for-all and what is a first-class board in one country is coded differently from the same class in another. Probably the best way to deal with the subject is to invent our own classes as follows:

Class 1. Practically free from all defects on both surfaces apart from a few small sound knots up to 5mm. ($\frac{3}{16}$in.) diameter, no worm holes, no joints unless they are reasonably matched for grain and colour, no discolouration.

Class 2. Sound knots up to 8mm. ($\frac{5}{16}$in.) diameter and natural discolouration permitted, also up to a maximum of three joints per face, and any loose knots which have been plugged.

Class 3. Knots up to 10mm. ($\frac{3}{8}$in.) diameter allowed, also plugs and all discolouration.

Class 4. All defects allowed: the boards are only required to be well glued.

As I have said, these classes do not relate to any particular board from any particular supplier but are included to give you some idea of what constitutes good, medium, and minimum qualities of plywood.

Sizes of plywood boards

The important point to bear in mind is that the first dimension quoted is the way the grain runs; thus, a board measuring 2440mm. (8ft.) × 1220mm. (4ft.) will have the grain of the exterior surfaces running parallel to the 2440mm. (8ft.) dimension, and is called a 'long grain' board. Its converse, a board measuring 1220mm. (4ft.) × 2440mm. (8ft.) would have its grain running parallel to its shorter dimension and would be called a 'cross-grain' board.

Boards are normally in any combination of the following sizes: 915mm. (3ft.); 1220mm. (4ft.); 1525mm. (5ft.); 1830mm. (6ft.); 2135mm. (7ft.); 2440mm. (8ft.); 2745mm. (9ft.); 3050mm. (10ft.); 3660mm. (12ft.) by 915mm. (3ft.); 1220mm. (4ft.); 1270mm. (4ft. 2in.); 1525mm. (5ft.); 1830mm. (6ft.).

Thicknesses range from 3mm. ($\frac{1}{8}$in.) to 25mm. (1in.) in one millimetre increments. 3mm. ($\frac{1}{8}$in.) ply is sometimes called 'aircraft ply' in Britain owing to its wartime use for that industry. Plywood which has over five veneers is usually referred to as 'multi-ply'.

Plastics laminates

More than any other single factor, plastics laminates have been responsible for introducing a new dimension into furniture design and interior decoration. It is now easy to bring gay colours into the furnishing scheme by bonding these laminates to wood cores, or if quiet elegance is required, then there are all the wood-grain patterns where a consistent figure with perfect matching is guaranteed. And as a most welcome bonus the laminates are resistant to heat and most household hazards, only needing a wipe to eliminate a catastrophe and to keep them clean.

To get down to technicalities, plastics laminates are made up as shown in Fig. 1. Here you can see that they consist of a number of layers of a fibrous material which is usually a cellulose-based paper treated with Phenol-formaldehyde resin. Upon the number of layers depends the thickness of the finished sheet, of course.

As shown, the bottom layer is coarse sanded to form a 'key' for any subsequent adhesive; then comes the main core of the 'base' layers. Over this is laid another paper which is printed with the required design or wood-

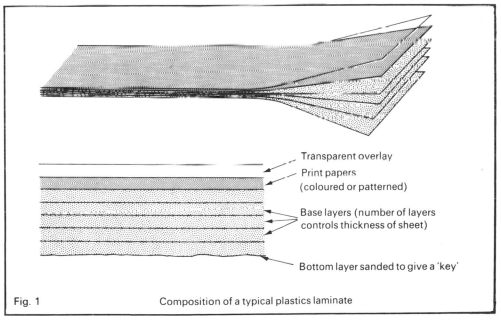

Transparent overlay

Print papers
(coloured or patterned)

Base layers (number of layers
controls thickness of sheet)

Bottom layer sanded to give a 'key'

Fig. 1   Composition of a typical plastics laminate

grain and treated with Melamine-formaldehyde. Finally, this is covered with an overlay of specially-treated paper which becomes transparent under heat-pressure treatment. The general properties are as follows:

Resistance to dry heat. Normally, laminates can withstand surface temperatures up to 180 deg.C. (356 deg.F.) for short periods although there may be a slight dulling of the glossy surface. If it is inevitable that hot cooking utensils will be stood on a plastics laminate, make sure that it is for a few seconds only.

However, temperatures up to 120 deg.C. (248 deg.F.) can be borne for several hours. When using plastics laminates in a fire surround, do bear in mind that not only will the laminate grow hot, but so will the core to which it is bonded. This can lead to cracking and splitting and the maximum permissible temperature in these conditions is 60 deg.C. (140 deg.F.).

Although normal laminates have good resistance to cigarette burns, if any particular area is continually subjected to this treatment (as on the counter-top of a cocktail bar) it would be worth investing in a 'cigarette-proof' laminate which has a metal foil layer incorporated to take care of this problem.

In addition, plastics laminates are resistant to boiling water and, in fact, test samples are required to be immersed in boiling, distilled water for two hours without showing any deterioration.

Resistance to abrasive wear is difficult to establish from the point of view of domestic usage as there can be no standard amount of use. But without doubt laminates can stand up to normal wear and tear for many years although the cutting action of knives or similar edge tools can score them. As a general practice it is wise not to overdo rubbing them with scouring powders, leaving it until absolutely necessary. In the majority of cases stains can be wiped off with a damp cloth anyway.

Here is a table showing stain resistance to some common materials:

Can be wiped off	acetone, household ammonia, amyl acetate (as used in nail-polish remover), carbon tetrachloride (dry-cleaning fluid), detergent, mustard, petrol, shoe polishes of all kinds, urine, wax crayon.
May cause a temporary stain which can be removed by light abrasion	alcohol (and methylated spirits), citric acid (orange, lemon and lime juice), coffee, fountain pen inks (washable), malt vinegar, milk, tea.
Can cause a permanent stain if left on surface: remove immediately	ballpoint pen ink, berry juices, caustic alkalis (as used for cleaning toilets), household bleaches, hydrochloric and other acids.

Sizes for plastics laminates are:
762mm. (2ft. 6in.) × 1525mm. (5ft.)
762mm. (2ft. 6in.) × 1830mm. (6ft.)
762mm. (2ft. 6in.) × 2135mm. (7ft.)
762mm. (2ft. 6in.) × 2440mm. (8ft.)
762mm. (2ft. 6in.) × 2745mm. (9ft.)
762mm. (2ft. 6in.) × 3050mm. (10ft.)
915mm. (3ft.) × 1525mm. (5ft.)
915mm. (3ft.) × 1830mm. (6ft.)
915mm. (3ft.) × 2135mm. (7ft.)
915mm. (3ft.) × 2440mm. (8ft.)
1220mm. (4ft.) × 1830mm. (6ft.)
1220mm. (4ft.) × 2440mm. (8ft.)
1220mm. (4ft.) × 2745mm. (9ft.)
1220mm. (4ft.) × 3050mm. (10ft.)
1525mm. (5ft.) × 3660mm. (12ft.)

Thicknesses available are: 0.5mm. ($\frac{1}{50}$in.); 0.6mm. ($\frac{1}{40}$in.); 0.8mm. ($\frac{1}{32}$in.); 1.0mm. ($\frac{1}{25}$in.); 1.2mm. ($\frac{3}{64}$in.—the most common thickness); 1.3mm. ($\frac{1}{20}$in.); 1.5mm. ($\frac{1}{16}$in.); 2.5mm. ($\frac{1}{10}$in.); 3.0mm. ($\frac{1}{8}$in.), 6.35mm. ($\frac{1}{4}$in.).

A word about buying in bulk. If you will be needing about a dozen sheets, it is worth buying them all from the same batch. As with wallpaper, colours can vary slightly from batch to batch.

Chapter 5
Some Useful Timbers

Here is a list of some of the timbers you are likely to encounter, together with relevant comments. They are shown alphabetically, regardless of whether they are hardwoods or softwoods; I have not shown the weight of each timber as it is not important in this context.

Name of timber

Comment

Abura (from Equatorial Africa). Hardwood.

If I were asked what timber approximates to the ideal cabinet-making wood, this would be high on the list. It is a uniform light brown colour with a slight reddish tinge and the sapwood and heartwood are practically indistinguishable. You will need sharp tools to avoid a slightly fibrous finish, but it stains and polishes superbly. Seasons well and consistently.

Afara (from West Africa). Hardwood.

This is a straw colour and could be said to resemble light oak. Unfortunately, the grain is often irregular and can split unless pre-bored before nailing or screwing. Polishes and stains well, but look out for possible discolouration which may occur during seasoning.

Afrormosia (most parts of Africa). Hardwood.

Has a brownish-yellow colour with darker streaks; a good timber to work although the grain tends to be variable.

Agba (Central Africa). Hardwood.

Another good cabinet timber although it is sometimes rather gummy. Polishes well. Yellowish-pink to light reddish-brown. Has a nice, straight grain and a fine texture.

Beech (Great Britain, Europe, Yugoslavia). Hardwood.

One of the most pleasant woods to work, as it has a close grain with a fine, even texture. Its unpleasant habit of twisting and warping if used as flat timber prevents its use as a cabinet-making wood. However, it is ideal for chair and table frames, particularly upholstered ones as it will hold tacks right up to its edges. As a turnery wood it is unsurpassed.

It can vary from off-white to straw-yellow in colour; a type called 'steamed beech' sometimes has a pinkish tinge.

Seasoning can be tricky and one must let it take its time to avoid such hazards as splits. Although it stains readily, it is not too responsive to French, wax or oil polishing.

British Columbian Pine (British Columbia). Also known as B.C. Pine, Douglas Fir, Oregon Pine, Red Pine, Red Fir, Yellow Fir. Softwood.

This is a magnificent tree and commonly grows to a height of 76m. (250ft.) with a butt diameter of 1.5m (5ft.). Consequently it is one of the few remaining sources of long, wide boards.

It works beautifully although sharp tools are needed; pre-boring is advised for nailing and screwing. As it does not shrink much during seasoning and is generally stable it is ideal for such frameworks as doors and windows, but these must be well painted for exterior use.

The wood really has two colours—the sapwood, which rarely exceeds 50mm. (2in.), is yellow while the heartwood is reddish-yellow to brown. Hence the names 'yellow fir' and 'red fir'.

Gedu Nohor (East and West Africa). Hardwood.

One of the many African hardwoods which are growing in popularity. A good cabinet-making wood but quite often with an interlocked grain which makes it difficult to plane. Because of this feature it closely resembles sapele (q.v.). (Not recommended for wood turnery.)

It polishes and stains extremely well and

is a warm reddish-brown colour. Available in convenient sizes.

Guarea (West Africa). Hardwood.

Reddish-brown in colour, and quite often has an attractive mottled figure. Works well but one sometimes meets a gummy board. Polishes well, as the timber has a fine, even texture.

Idigbo (Central and West Africa). Hardwood.

A strong timber, and used in its own country for such items as bridge work and railway rolling stock. It is yellow-brown in colour and has a coarse grain which can be tricky in some boards. However, it normally works well and stains and polishes excellently. (A good turnery wood.)

Iroko (West Africa). Often called 'African Teak'. Hardwood.

Medium to dark brown in colour with an open grain which often requires filling before applying polish, to which it responds well.
Rather hard work to plane, as it often has patches of cross-grain. Its main advantage is its strength and durability. Excellent material for boat building.

Makore (West Africa). Hardwood.

A deservedly popular hardwood which is quite straightforward to work except that planing can sometimes be difficult owing to interlocked grain. It is not, therefore, a good wood for turnery.
Can vary in colour from pale, reddish-brown to almost a purple-brown so you will have to choose boards most carefully for colour-matching. Stains and polishes excellently.

Oaks (American). Hardwood.

The American oaks comprise two main kinds, the 'white' and the 'red'. When available they can be had in good sizes and they are consistently reliable timbers, very strong but with little if any figure. They work well and take stain and polish readily.

Oaks (British, European, Japanese).
Hardwood.

British oak, though strong and practically everlasting, is problematic and every plank brings its own difficulties. These include wild- and cross-grain, shakes that do not reveal themselves until the wood is cut, and knots. All these, however, give the timber a distinctive figure which can be most beautiful when polished.

European oaks, and Japanese oaks, are altogether milder in texture and more easily worked—in fact Japanese oaks may be considered one of the best cabinet woods available.

Obeche (West Africa).
Also called Nigerian
whitewood, white
mahogany, wawa.
Hardwood.

This is a wood that is both light in weight and colour—pale straw, in fact.

The wood is very soft and easily bruised and its main use can only be for non-structural members, such as drawer stuff and cabinet backs. Most of the timber is straight-grained and very easy to work but occasionally one comes across some which has a 'roey' figure due to overlapping and interlocking grain. This can be troublesome to work although when polished it looks attractive.

Because of its open texture the timber takes stain and polishes well, but a good filler is needed to fill the grain.

Parana pine (South
America).
Softwood.

One of the most widely sold timbers in Great Britain today. It has a nice, even texture and straight grain and works easily; however, it does have the defect of being rather soft. Normally only available in narrow widths.

One disadvantage is that it is a rather nondescript, featureless timber to stain and polish. You must look out for the pronounced reddish streaks which occur at random and can ruin any attempt at a natural finish. Other than this the general colour is a pale straw for sapwood or medium brown for heartwood.

**Ramin (East Indies).
Hardwood.**

Another very popular timber in Britain—in fact, almost all the mouldings sold in Do-It-Yourself stores are ramin.

As a cabinet wood it is very acceptable—its strength is adequate and the colour is a uniform pale yellow which stains and polishes very easily. It does have a moderately coarse texture which makes it difficult to get tight, close-fitting joints, but on the other hand it is straight-grained and easy to work.

The rather unpleasant odour of the freshly sawn timber disappears as it dries; beware of splinters as they can cause painful irritation.

**Sapele (West Africa).
Hardwood.**

A hard and close-grained timber much used for veneer. Rather difficult to work owing to the interlocked grain which gives the wood its characteristic, roey stripe. Takes polish well, but stain is absorbed unevenly.

**Scots Pine
(Scandinavia, Russia,
Scotland). Also called
Red Baltic pine, Scots fir,
red pine, red deal, yellow
deal.
Softwood.**

This is the universally used 'deal' employed in building joinery, house and shop fitting, kitchen furniture and general woodwork.

The timber is light in weight, pale straw in colour and easily worked. Owing to the open grain, fine joints are difficult to cut. It is marketed in several grades, and the faults to look out for are mainly those shown in Fig. 1, especially knots, which should be firmly embedded in the surrounding wood fibres.

The usual finish is paint or enamel, but a clear varnish can be used to enhance the natural run of the grain and even the knots—hence the vogue for 'knotty pine' furniture and panelling.

**Utile (West Africa).
Hardwood.**

A close relative of both gedu nohor and sapele, this is a recognized cabinet-making wood. It too has the interlocked grain of its relatives, probably to a more marked degree which makes it difficult to plane and glass-paper. Not a wood for turnery.

The heartwood is a reddish-brown, in some cases purplish-brown, while the sapwood is a light brown. Difficult to stain uniformly, but polishes well.

Whitewood (Britain, Canada, U.S.A.). Properly Spruce *(Picea abies)*. Softwood.

A timber that lives up to its name, as its colour is a creamy white.

It is not a strong timber from a constructional viewpoint, but can be used for shelving, cupboards, benches, tables and the like. Owing to its comparative softness the wood tends to be woolly when worked and requires sharp tools.

Defects

Fig. 1 overleaf shows the defects likely to be found when buying timber. As you will appreciate, there are enough of these to make it highly advisable for you to inspect the stuff before buying it. Also included are charts showing the metric sizes of both hardwoods and softwoods, Fig. 2.

Hardwood	Softwood											Boards	
					Widths (mm)							Face sizes	Thickness
Length from 1.8mm rising by 100mm increments	Length (metres)	75	100	125	150	175	200	225	250	300		(mm)	(mm)
	1.8	16										915	3.2
Width from 150mm	2.1	19										1220	5.0
rising by 10mm	2.4	22										1525	6.5
or 25mm increments	2.7	25										1830	8.0
Thicknesses : 19mm	3.0	32										2135	9.5
25mm	3.3	38										2440	12.5
32mm	3.6	44										2745	16.0
38mm	3.9	50										3050	19.0
50mm	4.2	63										3660	22.0
63mm	4.5	75											25.5
75mm	4.8	100											32.0
100mm	5.1	150											35.0
125mm	5.4	200											38.0
thereafter by 25mm	5.7	250											41.0
increments	6.0	300											44.5
	6.3	Thickness (mm)											47.5

Fig. 2 The trade sizes of hardwoods, softwoods, and boards shown in metric dimensions. The tinted area in the softwood section shows the sizes available.

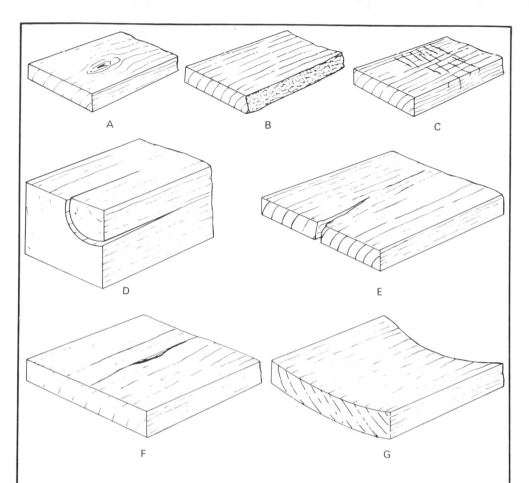

Fig. 1 Defects in timber. **A** avoid timber containing knots, if possible. Cut out dead knots, which have a black ring around them. **B** shows a waney edge which is sometimes left on hardwoods. It consists of bark and sapwood both of which must be removed. **C** illustrates felling or compression shakes and the parts containing them will have to be cut out. **D** is a 'cup' shake caused by the heart wood drying out more quickly than the rest, and it will have to be discarded. **E** must also be cut away as it is an 'end' shake although sometimes you can saw lengthwise to eliminate it. **F** is a 'shake' which can either extend part-way through the board or penetrate it completely. In both cases the affected area must be cut away. **G** shows a warped board. If the warping is crosswise as shown, the board will have to be cut into narrow strips lengthwise: if the warping is lengthwise, however, the board can be sawn into short lengths across it.

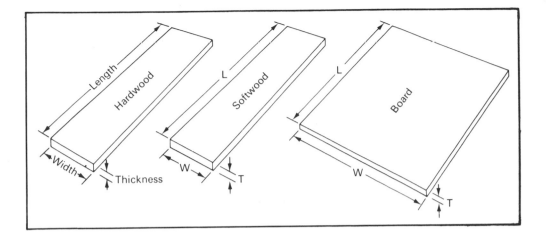

Be sure you know the implications of 'nominal sizes' and 'finished sizes' for timber as many a woodworker has had to alter his design because he was not aware of the difference. A simple example should suffice to show the significance. If you order a piece of softwood 25mm. × 50mm. (1in. × 2in.)—the length is immaterial—then those dimensions are the nominal sizes of the wood as it leaves the saw. Obviously you cannot use it in this condition for furniture or anything which requires polishing or painting, so you ask for it to be 'planed all round' (PAR). This is where bad mistakes can occur because, after planing, the finished size will only be, say, 22mm. × 47mm. ($\frac{7}{8}$in. × 1$\frac{7}{8}$in.)—the missing 3mm. ($\frac{1}{8}$in.) has been lost in planing. So do bear this in mind when setting out your design.

Chapter 6
Finishes for Contemporary Furniture

The paint finish

The uncharitable will say that a painted finish is the only one which can be used on some of the mediocre timber that we have to use nowadays! No doubt there is a certain amount of truth in that view; it is certainly true that you will invariably have to use woods that do not match for colour or for grain and the only way to achieve any kind of uniformity is to use paint.

Further, even the most enthusiastic advocate of hardboards and chipboards would not claim that their untreated surfaces could remotely be considered attractive. So, unless you are going to veneer them, cover them with a plastics laminate or use some such expedient, the only finish left is paint.

As a matter of interest, I recall that some years ago there was an attempt to produce coloured hardboards by introducing colour during the manufacturing process. Those I saw were dull reds and browns and not very appealing; there seems to be no mention of them in trade advertising so one presumes that the idea was abandoned.

I shall have to assume throughout that you have glasspapered the work ready for painting, and there are a few points worth mentioning about this. You will, of course, work from the coarsest grade of paper down to the finest —personally I use a power sander for the coarsest grades to get the rough stuff off and use a sanding block for the final glasspapering. It is most important to glasspaper *with* the grain and not across it, and this applies equally to powered as well as hand sanding. This does mean that the type of disc sander that you insert into the chuck of your power drill is not recommended as a moment's thought will demonstrate that the rotary motion of the disc is bound to cut across the grain. It is quite astonishing how difficult it is to get rid of sanding scratches across the grain and how much they show up, when polished, if you do not.

If a sanding block is used, make sure it is the proper kind. The best is a block of cork suitably sized for your hand; the next best is a block of wood which has a layer of thick felt glued to its face; the worst is any odd scrap of wood you can lay your hands on. The reason for the choice is that the face of the block must have a slight resiliency to accommodate high and low spots which occur in all woodwork. Without this resiliency, the glass-paper will only abrade the high spots and will eventually wear itself away in patches and even rip across.

It goes without saying that all blemishes such as holes and splits have to be filled with a wood stopping which is not the same as a wood filler. Brummer stoppings, which can be obtained in colours to match various woods, or Rawlplug Plastic Wood, are the types to use. When these have been applied and sanded down, brush off all loose dust with a soft brush.

Knots

Knots present a special problem as, unless they are specially treated, they will 'bleed' resin through the paint covering and will eventually blister and push the paint film off.

The traditional way is to paint them with Patent Knotting. Each knot, plus its immediate surrounding area, should be painted with two coats of Knotting with about half-an-hour's interval between each application. You will find an artist's large size brush best for this.

This treatment is followed by applying a coat of pink primer to the wood-work, paying particular attention to the crevices around the joints. Always leave a priming coat as long as you can to dry before applying an undercoat, but once you have painted on the undercoat, then the first finishing coat should be applied within 24 hours—in other words, while the undercoat is still slightly tacky even though it may feel dry.

Quicker method

The foregoing is the conventional procedure; there is, however, another method which is quicker and more effective.

This is to dispense with the Patent Knotting and pink primer and to paint the whole of the woodwork with Aluminium Wood Primer, which should not be confused with aluminium paint. This will itself seal the knots and prevent them bleeding and also act as a first-class priming coat. It has another advantage in that it is about the same consistency as milk and very easy to apply. Pink primer, on the other hand, is not, and can very soon develop into a wrist-aching business!

Many people believe that an undercoat is unnecessary in these days of advanced paint technology and that the finishing coats can follow the primer. For interior work, such as bedroom fitments and furniture, I am inclined to agree with them, but for exterior work and for woodwork which will be exposed to damp and condensation (as in the kitchen or bathroom) I think an undercoat is desirable.

Each coat needs lightly glasspapering when it has dried—just enough to remove any 'nibs' (specks of dust) and to provide a key for ensuing coats. It is worth bearing in mind that it is a good idea to sweep out the workshop to get rid of dust which could be kicked up while you are working; remember, too, that woollen clothing which harbours dust is definitely not recommended.

To achieve a high gloss finish you will probably need to apply two or three finishing coats, glasspapering lightly between each application.

Gloss finish

If you have a surface which you want to be flawless, completely and perfectly smooth, perhaps my own experience may be of interest.

Once, years ago, I was the proud possessor of a wooden-built boat which I used to paint meticulously, using all the traditional and conventional methods and materials. But still I could not achieve those gleaming white topsides seen in paint advertisements. Until, one day, I happened to be in the boatyard watching some professionals do the job.

Using broad-bladed flexible palette knives they were spreading a butter-consistency white stopping all over the topsides. When they had finished and before they had even begun to apply the paint, there was the ideal surface to paint on—matt, flawless, smooth, and obviously ready when painted to reflect anything that came along.

Now, if there is a door, a bed-head, or a table top to paint I adopt the same procedure. The first step is to glasspaper it smooth, then to apply a coat of aluminium wood primer. When this is dry, spread on the stopping. Usually, a spreader is supplied with the material but if not, buy a flexible palette knife with a blade at least a 100mm. (4in.) wide.

It is an ideal way to obtain a really good surface on chipboard, and it is handy, too, for filling in the raw edges of chipboard or plywood where the material has crumbled away due to sawing, planing or the like.

Hardboard

Before anything is done with hardboard it needs to be 'conditioned', a process which is described on page 74.

Painting hardboard is straightforward enough if one remembers that instead of either of the primers already described, a hardboard primer should be used which is specially formulated for the job.

Next there is the vexed question of whether to paint the back of the hardboard. If one is using it in an atmosphere where there is a good deal of condensation or damp, as there would be in a kitchen or a bathroom, then the back should definitely be painted with the primer and at least one finishing coat. This will prevent any bowing which could be caused by moisture getting into the unprotected back of the boards.

If large sheets are being used in a comparatively dry atmosphere—for a built-in wardrobe fitment, for example—it would still be wise to paint the backs. But for small pieces, say up to 300 sq. mm. (1 sq. ft.), it should not be necessary.

Once you have made this decision, and applied the hardboard primer, follow the standard painting procedure described, but omitting the primer.

Polyurethane lacquer

This is, of course, the favourite finish for the home woodworker and under-standably so as a good result is practically guaranteed if one follows a commonsense and straightforward sequence of actions. To avoid pitfalls, here is a non-technical outline of its characteristics and behaviour.

Generally, the lacquer can be described as a tolerant one in that it can be applied, and will remain, over virtually any other paint or lacquer. However, it has three principal enemies—moisture, oil, and the ballpoint pen.

The moisture referred to can be present in the bristles of the brush or on the surface of the wood, and it must be got rid of at all costs. This means that timber with a high moisture content must not be used until it has dried to an acceptable level (12%–14%). Also, brush bristles must be bone-dry and if you suspect they are damp, dip them in methylated spirit (wood alcohol) and twirl them round. As the spirit evaporates it will take the moisture with it. The results of moisture being present are weak bonding to the timber, or under-curing.

Oil, in this context, also includes grease which can result from too much handling of the timber. The best way to get rid of this is to wipe over the wood with white spirit and this is particularly desirable in the case of teak, which is greasy by nature. It is because of the lacquer's intolerance of oil that oil stains cannot be used for staining, only water or naphtha stains.

Ballpoint pen ink can mark the finish ineradicably so if you have the combination of Polyurethane-polished furniture and children, do not intro-duce the latter to ballpoint pens!

Although the time to touch-dryness can be as little as ten minutes and to handling without marking about an hour, the film does not finish curing for several days or even a week. This is something to be borne in mind because premature re-coating can result in pin-holes or minute bubbles appearing in the second coat; these are caused by the solvents in the first coat continuing to escape. The minimum safe period between coats is about six hours if conditions are good, but allow eight if in doubt.

Types of Polyurethane lacquer

There are two types of Polyurethane lacquer, the two-pack kind, and the one-pack. Of the two, I prefer the former as I think that it does give just that extra toughness to the finish.

In the two-pack type, one can is the base liquid and the other can is the hardener. I recommend that you mix the liquids in the proportions advised by the manufacturer; although there is a little tolerance one way or the other you can ruin the finish by being careless about it. And remember that the mixing must be done thoroughly to ensure proper curing.

Although it is referred to as a 'two-pack' lacquer you will probably find that there is a third can containing thinners, which can also be employed for brush cleaning. The pot-life of the liquids when mixed is about a day and during this time you can thin or thicken the mixture up. The shelf-life of the individual cans is virtually unlimited if they are properly sealed and protected from frost.

Polishing step-by-step

Now let us go through a typical project step-by-step, assuming that the woodwork is standing there well glasspapered and ready to be polished. These, then, are the various stages to go through.

1. The optimum temperature for polishing is about 20 deg.C. (68 deg.F.), and the atmosphere should be reasonably dry and free from damp or condensation. Check to see if these conditions are met.

2. Clean up the bench and the workshop so that you can cut down the amount of dust you might make airborne while working. Also, avoid dust-harbouring clothing such as woollens.

3. Inspect the woodwork and wipe over any likely greasy patches with a fluff-free cloth dampened with white spirit.

4. If the wood grain is to be filled, bearing in mind that the lacquer itself has high grain-filling qualities, do not use the oil-bound grain fillers which you would normally buy or you will get poor bonding if not outright failure. You must use the special fillers made for the job and this could mean contacting the manufacturer for advice.

5. If the wood is to be stained, avoid oil stains for the same reasons given under **4**. Water stains, naphtha stains or spirit stains are all suitable, however. If, for example, you want to tint the stain to give a warm shade, mix a little spirit dye into clear shellac and brush this on when the original stain is dry.

6. Assuming that you have mixed the two-pack lacquer (or the one-pack) and allowed it to stand for ten minutes, apply it with a good quality varnish brush which is clean and free from any sediment from previous use. Do not over-brush and introduce air bubbles, but try to float the lacquer on in a thin film.

7. Two coats are usually sufficient, so allow the first coat six—eight hours to cure and then de-nib it. This simply means lightly glasspapering it with the finest abrasive paper to remove such unwanted materials as tiny dust particles, small hairs, and sundry insects which seem to be drawn inexorably towards any freshly lacquered surface.

8. Apply the second coat within 24 hours of the first so that although the first will have partially cured, it will still 'key' into the second one.

9. If you want a satin or similar matt finish you must allow the second coat to cure for 24 hours. Then flat it down with the finest grade of steel wool dipped in furniture wax or a good furniture polish; rub lightly in the direction of the grain until you achieve the effect you want. Do make sure that no tiny particles of the steel wool break off and become embedded in the wax, which can happen quite easily in awkward corners and around mouldings, as the steel particles may eventually rust and cause unsightly stains.

Finally, clean off the surface with a soft, dry, fluff-free cloth.

Teak oil

This is an oil which gives a finish similar in appearance to that of linseed oil except that it has better resistance to marking.

Application is simple. Apply it liberally with a brush, working across the grain and allow about half an hour for the timber to absorb it. Then wipe off the surplus with a cloth. Drying time before applying a second coat should be overnight and the second coat must be a lighter one brushed along the grain. Avoid trying to build up a coat on the surface as teak is not the type of oil to use for this purpose and you will simply be faced with removing, and wasting, the excess.

Allow the oil quite a time to dry thoroughly before attempting to get a matt finish—at least a day, and preferably two days. Then you can lightly rub the surface along the grain with the finest steel wool and wax as already described.

The 'elbow grease' polishes

These are the names I call the linseed oil, petroleum jelly 'Vaseline', and wax finishes as the final result depends as much on hard rubbing as on the materials.

The linseed oil finish. You will need equal parts of boiled linseed oil and pure turpentine, (although best quality white spirit is an acceptable substitute). Mix them together thoroughly and if you want to speed up drying, which is highly desirable, add terebine driers at the rate of one teaspoonful to 0.3 litre ($\frac{1}{2}$ pt.) of linseed oil. Do not confuse terebine with terebene, as the latter is used medicinally and is not the same thing at all!

Apply the liquid with a cloth or a stiff brush, working across the grain. It helps if the mixture is kept warm by immersing the container in hot water. Remember that it is inflammable and should not be exposed, for instance, to a naked flame.

Allow a few hours for the mixture to be absorbed and then wipe off the surplus. Leave the work for a couple of days and then repeat the process. In fact, you may have to make three or four applications before you get a good result. Finally, rub the surface vigorously along the grain with a soft cloth wrapped around a brick or a similar weighty object: this is where the elbow grease is needed!

The surface will, of course, be water-resistant because of the oil content, but it will be liable to marking. To make it more resistant you will need to give additional applications periodically, always rubbing them well in. Unfortunately, the surface will be badly marked by heat or spirits but at least one can always work up the finish to get rid of marks.

The 'Vaseline' finish. This is applied in much the same way and is particularly suitable for close-grained woods such as iroko, oak, rosewood, and teak. Rub it well into the grain with a cloth, allow it 24 hours or so for absorption and then wipe off the surplus and buff it up with a clean, dry, soft cloth. It gives a water-resistant surface which is also more resistant to marking than linseed oil, but it is still very susceptible to heat and spirits damage.

The wax finish. Perhaps, one of the most attractive there is as it has a slight sheen which improves over the years, particularly if it is well buffed up from time to time. You could make up your own mixture but some ingredients will be very difficult to obtain and it is a slow business. A high quality proprietary furniture wax is more convenient and gives good results.

The first step is to give the woodwork a couple of coats of clear French polish (shellac), each coat being lightly glasspapered down. This is to give the wood a protective sealing coat which will prevent dirt being forced into the grain by periodic rubbing over the years.

A shoe brush is ideal for applying the first coat of wax, which should be a heavy one. Work the brush in all directions but finish off by stroking it lightly along the grain. Now leave the polish to harden, overnight for example, and then buff it up with a clean, soft cloth.

The same remarks apply regarding surface marking as for the two other finishes and, of course, periodic light applications of wax polish will greatly enhance the appearance.

Chapter 7
Adhesives

From a rough count I have just made from a directory of adhesives I see that there are about 97 different kinds! So there is definitely good reason to feel rather bewildered at the vast array of brand names that appear in trade literature and magazines. However, we can narrow the field down drastically as many of the adhesives are unlikely to interest us—those that bond brake linings to metal, for instance. In fact, there are only seven different types which really concern us:

1. Animal and fish glues (Scotch glue).
2. Casein glues.
3. Contact adhesives.
4. Epoxies.
5. Polyvinyl acetate (PVA) adhesives.
6. Resorcinol formaldehyde (RF) adhesives.
7. Urea-formaldehyde (UF) adhesives.

And of these only five (numbers 1, 3, 4, 5 and 6) need ever appear in your workshop.

Animal glues

Animal and fish glues are those which have been used for centuries and are made from the otherwise unusable parts of dead animals and fish. One can at least say that animal glues have stood the test of time, although they have one defect—they cannot tolerate damp or moist conditions and will sooner or later fail. However, this defect does have a useful corollary in that if you should make a mistake, in veneering for example, you can wipe off the glue, allow the parts to dry, and start again. This kind of glue can be bought in tubes and cans for small jobs but work of any size will need a bag of glue granules, or a thin cake which must be broken up before melting.

The glue should be heated in a double-walled glue-pot which has a hot water jacket to keep the glue hot. Be very careful not to boil the glue or it will be rendered useless; it should be just hot enough so that when you dip a wooden rod into it, it will run off as a thin syrup in one continuous stream. If it is too cold, the syrup will be too thick to run freely; if it is too hot, the stream will break into beads. Also the glue must never be allowed to 'chill' by being applied to wood that is cold or damp, otherwise the bond will be useless. It follows, then, that for successful gluing, the temperature of the workshop must be warm (20 deg.C. or 68 deg.F.) and the wooden parts should be warmed before the glue is applied.

Joints must be cramped and allowed time for the glue to set which, to be safe, should be overnight. Excess glue can be wiped off with a damp rag while it is still fluid.

Owing to their complicated preparation, animal glues are worthy of inclusion only if you contemplate doing a lot of delicate veneering work, or repairs to old furniture.

Casein glues

Casein glues are derived from milk protein and, while strong for indoor use, have poor resistance to damp, water, and mould growth. They are normally supplied in powder form which has to be mixed with water. Joints need to be cramped and the glue may stain some woods although any excess can be wiped off with a damp rag. Do not allow the temperature to rise above 18 deg.C. (64 deg.F.) or the adhesive will not set.

Contact adhesives

Contact adhesives are the ones used to bond plastics laminates to wood, or latex and plastics foams to wood. The usual method is to coat both surfaces and allow the adhesive to dry; as soon as the surfaces meet the bond is formed. Cramping is unnecessary and one can normally apply hand pressure to create the adhesion. The manufacturer's instructions must be followed.

These adhesives are not suitable for the normal fixing of one wooden part to another as the bond will tend to 'creep' when stress is applied. Nevertheless you will need two cans in your kit—one of the type for fixing plastics laminates, and one for sticking down fabrics, foams, and other upholstery materials.

Epoxies

For real strength and resistance to almost any conceivable hazard, epoxy resins are my choice. They will bond pretty well everything to everything else with the exception of PVC plastics and are ideal for fixing wood to metal, or wood to glass. Certainly to be added to your kit.

Epoxies are supplied in a two-part form, one component being the resin and the other the hardener and these must be thoroughly mixed in the proportions recommended by the manufacturer. The two main causes of failure with epoxies are insufficient mixing and incomplete cleaning of the surfaces to be joined. Cleaning must be very thorough as the adhesive is intolerant of the slightest trace of grease, oil, or dirt. Hence the surfaces should be completely free of these and it is worthwhile wiping them over with a degreasing agent such as carbon tetrachloride (stain remover).

Epoxies can be obtained which set in five minutes or 48 hours! Heat is the determining factor and if the joint can be warmed in some way, by the air from a hair drier for instance, or by standing it near an electric fire, setting will be greatly accelerated. But you will need to cramp the parts together while this is in progress.

Once set, the joint will be resistant to hot or cold water, heat, spirits, most chemicals and oils. There is, naturally, a snag which is that epoxies are expensive for the amateur to use except in comparatively small quantities. Excess can be removed with methylated spirits (wood alcohol).

PVA adhesives

PVA (Polyvinyl-acetate) adhesive is the general-purpose woodworking glue which has virtually displaced animal glues and is indispensable for our purposes. It is relatively cheap, requires no mixing, and is fool proof to apply as no special conditions are necessary.

While not as strong as the RF and UF adhesives, it is adequate for most work, although it should be remembered that it is not water-resistant. The initial 'set' takes about 20 minutes, which gives time for adjustments, and full curing takes approximately 24 hours. Cramps are needed during the setting period; excess glue can be wiped away with a damp rag.

Resorcinol-formaldehyde

Resorcinol-formaldehyde (RF) could be called the 'boatbuilder's' glue as it is ideal for completely water-resistant joints. This makes it equally suitable for outdoor garden furniture, of course.

The glue is supplied as a two-part pack which must be mixed strictly in accordance with the manufacturer's instructions, and joints have to be cramped while the adhesive sets, which takes four to six hours. It is really only necessary if you are undertaking outdoor woodwork.

Urea-formaldehyde

Urea-formaldehyde (UF) is used largely for plywood manufacture where specially heated presses and strictly controlled conditions allow fast production. Thus, there are two types of the adhesive, the hot-setting kind, which needs precisely controlled conditions, and the cold-setting one which is relevant here.

The adhesive is always a two-part pack, one being the resin and the other, the hardener. Apply them strictly in accordance with the manufacturer's instructions. Some have to be mixed, while others set by having one part coated with resin and the other part with the hardener. When the two are brought together, setting takes place. Allow four to six hours for this and bear in mind that cramps will be needed.

Such joints are probably the strongest of all and have good water-resistance. An added bonus is that these adhesives are gap-filling although the gaps must not be more than 0.05in. wide.

Opposite is a summary of the principal characteristics of each adhesive. **Note:** Animal glue, once mixed, should be used up in 12 hours; epoxy, RF and UF adhesives all have a long shelf life if properly sealed.

Using adhesives in upholstery

A good contact adhesive can be used for sticking either polyether or latex foams. The procedure is to apply a thin coat of adhesive to both surfaces and allow it to become 'touch-dry', which usually takes from ten to fifteen minutes. When the surfaces are brought together an immediate bond is formed which only needs firm hand pressure to complete it.

This characteristic of forming an immediate bond can be annoying if for one reason or another one wants to shuffle the pieces around before deciding on the final position. The new thixotropic contact adhesives allow fifteen to twenty minutes to do this and are, therefore, preferable to the ordinary adhesives.

It is always useful to have a tin of French chalk about so that you can sprinkle it over the glued bonds and hide any stickiness. Finally, latex foam has one enemy, direct light. Once it is covered with a fabric there is no danger, of course, but during working and certainly during storage, the foam should always be protected or moved away from direct light.

Name of adhesive

Characteristic	Animal	Casein	Contact	Epoxy	PVA	RF	UF
General strength	Good	Good	Very fair	Excellent	Good	Excellent	Excellent
Water resistance	Nil	Poor	Fair	Excellent	Poor	Excellent	Good
Damp resistance	Poor	Fair	Good	Excellent	Fair	Excellent	Good
Mould resistance	Poor	Fair	Good	Excellent	Good	Excellent	Excellent
Heat resistance	Nil	Good	Very fair	Excellent	Poor	Good	Good
Gap filling	Nil	Slight	Nil	Good	Nil	Good	Good
Hardening time	6–8 hrs.	4–6 hrs.	10–30 min.	5 min. to 48 hrs.	20–40 min.	6–8 hrs.	6–8 hrs.
Colour when dry	Light brown	Clear straw	Clear pale straw	Yellow	Clear	Opaque white	Opaque white
Liable to stain	No	Yes	No	No	No	Yes some woods	Yes some woods
Life in container or after mixing	2 or 3 months properly sealed	Up to 24 hrs.	Long if properly sealed	5 min. to 6 hrs. depending on type	Long if properly sealed	$\frac{1}{2}$ hr. to 4 hrs.	$\frac{1}{2}$ hr. to 4 hrs.

Chapter 8
Power Tools and Machines for the Workshop

The possibility of equipping your workshop with machines of one sort or another is something that should be borne in mind at the very outset of your woodworking career. All too often powered accessories and machines are acquired haphazardly with the result that one machine is overworked while another is hardly used.

This is not to say that you should go out one morning with a shopping list and order all the machines you are ever likely to need—a delightful thought!—but rather that there should be some kind of overall plan to govern purchases as and when you can afford them.

Many a woodworker has bought himself a very impressive power drill and set of drills thinking that by so doing he has done himself a good turn. In fact, all he has done is to provide himself with the mechanized facility for drilling thousands of holes of slightly different sizes and what woodworking job calls for that? Unless you want to make your own perforated hardboard, that is!

You will probably be able to tackle all of your hole-boring jobs for a long time with a hand drill and a brace and bit, while a power drill is not strictly necessary for this purpose. One proviso ought to be made, however, which is that a power drill which can be mounted in a vertical stand is a useful thing to have as it will enable you to drill holes which can be guaranteed to be at right angles to the surface being bored. If you do a lot of dowelled joints you can readily appreciate what a boon this can be. With a little practice and some care you can approximate to this with a hand drill lined up against a try square as a guide, but the vertical drill stand is undoubtedly a great help. Decide what kind of woodwork you intend to do first before wasting money on unnecessary equipment.

It is more likely, however, that you will buy a power tool as a power source for various accessories such as a circular saw, or sanders of various kinds. This is a much more worthwhile investment provided you appreciate that, while you can and should get good results, the best results come from heavier and more stable machines which are designed for a specific series of jobs.

Power tool accessories do score, of course, in certain kinds of wood-working where one has to take the machine to the work rather than bring the work to the machine. Such kinds of woodwork would include boat-building, caravan building, making outdoor garden sheds or greenhouses and could extend to installing built-in cupboards or fitments in the home. In all these instances it would be infuriating to have the machine to do the job and yet be unable to use it because it could not be brought to the work-site.

In addition to the power tool accessories, there is quite a range of portable appliances with their own built-in motors which do a similar range of jobs and can be freely moved about.

To sum up, then, we come to the following position where alternative tools are available for doing the same jobs:

Power tool accessories	Portable self-powered tools
Circular saw which can be used freehand or mounted on a saw bench	Self-powered circular saw
Jig saw attachment into which the power tool is inserted	Self-powered jig saw which is lighter and more manoeuvrable than the attachment opposite, but which basically does not do any more
Flexible sanding disc Foam rubber or plastics drum sander	No equivalent: bench models only No equivalent: bench models only
Orbital sander attachment Virtually the same as each other	Self-powered orbital sander
No equivalent, but milling attach-ments can be fitted to power tool to do moulding work	Self-powered router for trenching, grooving, rebating, moulding

Unfortunately, one maker's accessories do not necessarily fit another maker's power tool, so it is best to choose one manufacturer and stick to their products.

The power tool

This is usually rated by the chuck size (the largest diameter shank the chuck will hold) and this can be either 6mm. ($\frac{1}{4}$in.) or 10mm. ($\frac{3}{8}$in.); larger sizes are available on heavy-duty professional models.

Over the past few years the single speed drill has gradually been replaced by the two- or four-speed drill. In general, the appropriate speed for most woodworking jobs is 2,500 r.p.m.–3,000 r.p.m., but the lower speed of 1,000 r.p.m. is needed for lathe work when turning wood with a diameter greater than 50mm. (2in.); it is also needed for drilling in masonry.

Maintenance of the power tool has been reduced to a minimum and consists of dealing with two factors only—renewing the grease in the gearbox, and cleaning up the brushes.

It is difficult to say how often the grease should be changed as it depends on how much the tool is used, but every 200 hours can be taken as a rough guide. Clean out the old grease with a piece of pointed stick and re-pack with the grease recommended by the manufacturer.

To clean the brushes, wipe them with white spirit (turpentine substitute) and trim them if necessary with a piece of very fine abrasive paper. Do not overdo this or they will become mis-shapen. Be careful to note how they are fitted before removing them.

Drills

Fig. 1 shows a selection of the most useful types of drill for our purposes. The twist drill in Fig. 1A is primarily intended for drilling metal but can be, and often is, used for woodwork. Owing to the shallow angle of the nose, it is advisable to 'pop' (punch) a small hole or indentation to start the drill accurately and prevent its wandering. Such drills do have the disadvantage that when they are used in softwood a core of waste tends to build up and clog the threads, so the tool should be stopped from time to time and the threads of the drill cleaned out.

Fig. 1B shows an auger bit. These have a sharp spur on the tip so that they can be centred exactly and bore in any direction without wandering with the grain. Fig. 1C shows a dowel bit. These are similar to twist bits but in larger diameters to suit standard dowel sizes. Figs. 1D and E show a flat bit and a power bore bit. The former is a simple form of bit for boring large holes and has the advantage that it can easily be sharpened. The latter is for fast, accurate drilling of larger holes.

Circular saw

Whether self-powered or as an accessory to a separate power tool, this is about the most useful tool you can have. The heart of the tool is the saw blade and, as you see in Fig. 2, there are four main types. The combination

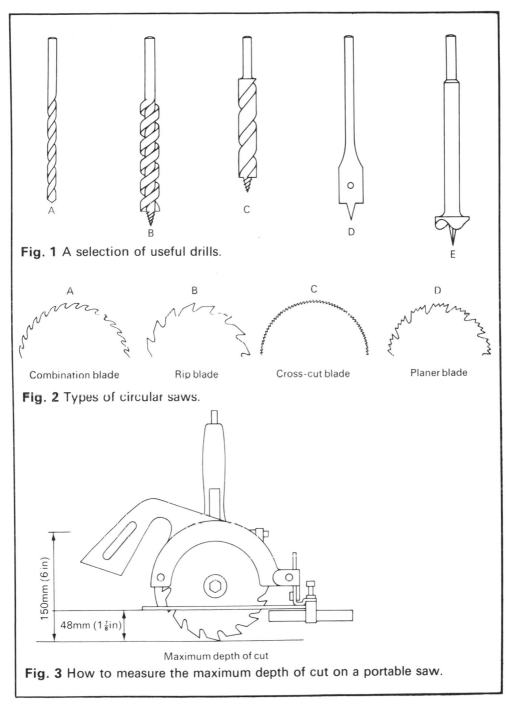

Fig. 1 A selection of useful drills.

Combination blade   Rip blade   Cross-cut blade   Planer blade

Fig. 2 Types of circular saws.

150mm (6 in)

48mm (1⅞in)

Maximum depth of cut

Fig. 3 How to measure the maximum depth of cut on a portable saw.

blade, as its name implies, is a general-purpose one and if you only use the saw infrequently it may well be the only blade you will need.

If you are called on to do a lot of cutting with the grain, the rip blade shown at Fig. 2B is the one to use. For the opposite job, cutting across the grain, employ the crosscut blade illustrated at Fig. 2C which has small, fine teeth to cut cleanly.

The planer blade, Fig. 2D, is rather more specialist in nature. It has no 'set' on its teeth and consequently is used where very fine, narrow cuts are necessary. It needs keeping sharp and should always be run at maximum speed.

Fig. 3 shows you how the maximum depth of cut is measured on a portable circular saw, bearing in mind that the largest diameter of blade is 150mm. (6in.). Always make sure that the blade guard on any circular saw you buy is operating properly—it is self-adjusting and falls automatically to cover those parts of the blade which are not in contact with the work.

In Fig. 4 you can see the various parts of the tool illustrated. The sole plate should be adjusted so that the blade just penetrates through the work and thus allows the greatest number of teeth to cut. Also shown in Figs. 5 and 6 are the use of the guide fence to retain a uniform width, making cuts at an angle by adjusting the sole plate and guide fence, and making a series of cuts side by side to form a groove.

Always make sure the saw is running at full speed before starting to cut, and when the cut is completed, switch off and allow the saw to stop before lifting it away from the work. Also, always keep the sole plate firmly and squarely bedded on to the wood. Blades must, of course, be kept sharp and if possible you should learn how to do this yourself. If not, you will almost certainly find that the tool suppliers will be able to offer this service.

The usefulness of the circular saw is greatly increased if it can be fitted into its own bench, and most manufacturers offer this facility. This is where buying the best one can afford really scores; while a good saw bench can be an inestimable boon, a bad one will drive you to desperation. The two principal faults that make a saw bench bad are poor construction and in-accuracy. Poor construction includes flimsy materials that bend and rob the saw bench of any pretence to rigidity, while inaccuracy includes tables that are not truly flat and clamps that do not give a positive fixing.

Before starting work, check that the saw blade is exactly at right angles to the saw table. As you can see from Fig. 7 the easiest way to do this is to rest a try square on the table with its blade lined up against the saw.

When using the fence, see that it is exactly parallel to the saw blade; if it is even slightly out of true the work could jam and the blade overheat. By far the best way is to insert a length of timber of the required width between the saw blade and the fence. If this is not possible, you will have to rely on a rule, but do be as exact as you can.

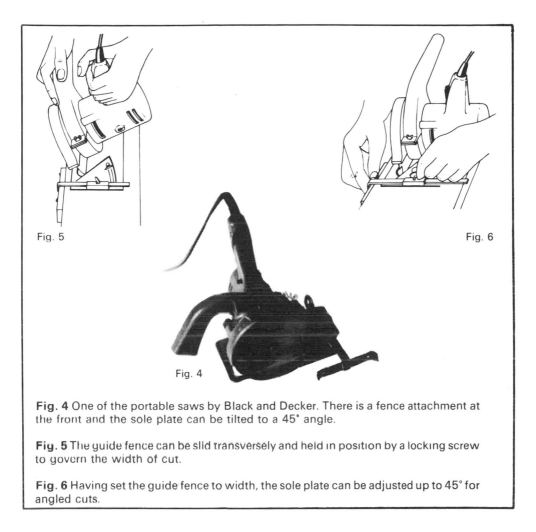

Fig. 5

Fig. 6

Fig. 4

Fig. 4 One of the portable saws by Black and Decker. There is a fence attachment at the front and the sole plate can be tilted to a 45° angle.

Fig. 5 The guide fence can be slid transversely and held in position by a locking screw to govern the width of cut.

Fig. 6 Having set the guide fence to width, the sole plate can be adjusted up to 45° for angled cuts.

Do not attempt to feed small pieces of wood into the saw blade or there could be a nasty accident. Make a push stick, Fig. 8, and use it to push the small stuff through. When crosscutting, arrange your hands equidistant from the blade, and well away from it, and push with equal force on each hand, Fig. 9.

Jig saw or 'Sabre saw'

This is shown in Fig. 10, and is used for cutting straight lines, or more particularly, small-radius curves and holes. As the blade is narrow, being

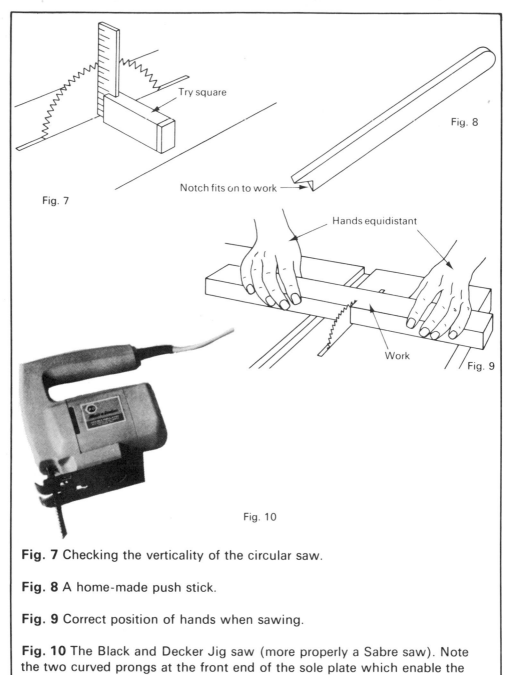

Fig. 7 Checking the verticality of the circular saw.

Fig. 8 A home-made push stick.

Fig. 9 Correct position of hands when sawing.

Fig. 10 The Black and Decker Jig saw (more properly a Sabre saw). Note the two curved prongs at the front end of the sole plate which enable the saw to be tilted for plunge cutting.

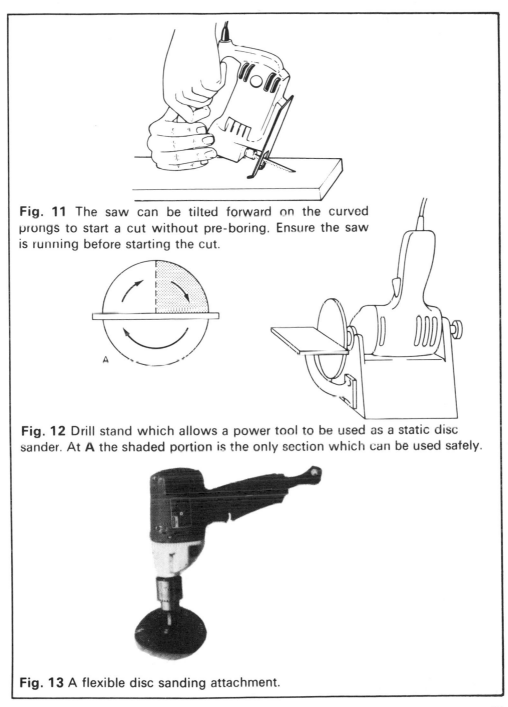

Fig. 11 The saw can be tilted forward on the curved prongs to start a cut without pre-boring. Ensure the saw is running before starting the cut.

Fig. 12 Drill stand which allows a power tool to be used as a static disc sander. At **A** the shaded portion is the only section which can be used safely.

Fig. 13 A flexible disc sanding attachment.

about 6mm. ($\frac{1}{4}$in.), quite sharp and intricate curves and shapes can be negotiated. In addition, cuts can be started in boards up to about 12mm. ($\frac{1}{2}$in.) or so thick without pre-boring by a technique known as 'plunge' cutting. This is shown in Fig. 11, and involves tilting the tool forward on to the curved fingers and then slowly lowering it backwards—the saw must be running before this is attempted, of course.

There are blades for cutting different materials such as metals and plastics laminates as well as the standard ones for timber and man-made boards. Once they are worn out they must be replaced as there is no question of their being re-sharpened.

The blade cuts on the up-stroke of an up-and-down movement of about 10mm. ($\frac{3}{8}$in.), consequently you will need to exert moderate pressure to keep the sole plate on the work.

Disc sander

The rigid type of this sander, Fig. 12, is also available as an attachment to a power tool. It is very handy for sanding end grain smooth and perfectly square.

Again, check that the face of the disc is at right angles to the table before starting work. You can only use one quarter of the entire disc, Fig. 12A, as the rotation follows the direction of the arrow and you will be unable to hold the work down on to the table.

The abrasive paper disc is glued to the face of the disc with the adhesive supplied by the manufacturer. Do not be tempted to use any other adhesive as when the paper is worn it will have to be peeled off and only a certain type of adhesive has this capacity. To spread the adhesive, apply it evenly to the backing disc while the tool is running, then switch off and let the disc stop before pressing the abrasive paper on firmly.

Flexible and drum sanders

A flexible sander disc seems to me the least vital of tools. As shown in Fig. 13, it consists of a flexible rubber disc to which an abrasive paper or cloth disc is fixed by means of a central screw.

What damns it in my opinion is the fact that it can so easily scratch or score a piece of woodwork, and any one who has had this experience will know how difficult it is to remove the mark. Wood is always sanded or glass-papered along the direction of the grain and, by virtue of its rotary motion, it is difficult for the flexible disc to do this. Fig. 14 shows you the wrong and the recommended way to use the tool, but even if it is used correctly,

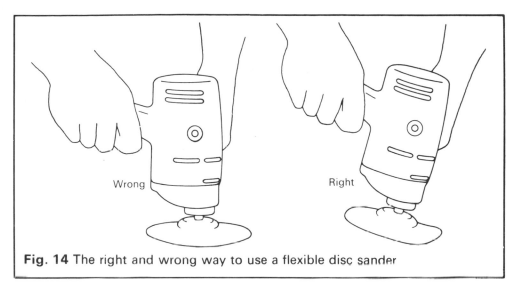

Wrong

Right

Fig. 14 The right and wrong way to use a flexible disc sander

it is fatally easy to score the surface. So, on all occasions, use the lightest possible pressure.

The drum sander, Fig. 15, is simply a foam rubber or foam plastics drum fitted with an abrasive paper 'tyre' which is glued in place with a similar adhesive to that used for the rigid disc sander.

It can be very useful indeed for sanding both concave and convex shapes, and for curves in general. Use it with as light a pressure as possible. Buy the best you can afford and if possible, test it in the shop. Cheap ones are often unbalanced and when they rotate at high speed they set up a vibration which could play havoc with the bearings of the power tool.

Orbital sander

This is so called because the abrasive paper is stretched over a cushioned pad which rotates in small circles about 10mm. ($\frac{3}{8}$in.) in diameter. It is a pleasant tool to use, and no downward pressure is really needed as its own weight is sufficient in most cases, but you will need to hold the side handle as well to guide it. It is intended for the finer stages of sanding only, and is not meant to remove appreciable amounts of wood.

Self-powered router

Even if you have a workshop full of expensive machines, this is one tool which can rapidly make itself indispensable. The router can be used to do the following:

1. Cut mortises,

2. Put the moulded edging on your work: the profile of the moulding depends on the shape of cutter you use,

3. Do the same job on a circular or elliptical shape.

4. Grooving and trenching.

5. Clearing away 'ground' timber: that is to say, it will remove waste wood to form a sunken recess—useful if you are making decorative carving.

6. You can use it freehand to cut out a pattern. With a little practice and a steady hand you could letter house name-boards, for instance.

7. With the aid of a special template you can cut dovetails easily and accurately.

Buy the best you can afford, as although routers are not cheap, a good one will greatly extend the range of your woodwork.

Fig. 16 shows a light-duty router capable of various jobs with the aid of the various fences, guides, and trammels which are supplied with it; if you care to experiment with making your own jigs it will undertake almost any job.

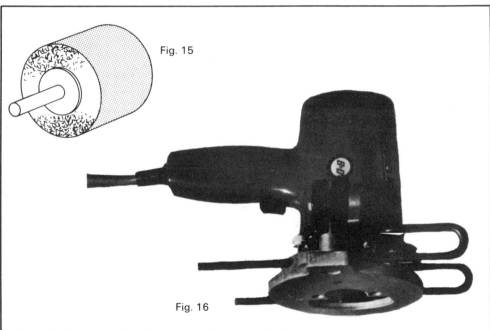

Fig. 15

Fig. 16

Fig. 15 Drum sander for use with power tool.

Fig. 16 One of the most versatile tools, the router. This is a lightweight one made by Black and Decker.

Machines for the workshop

Although the power tool accessories may be adequate for some woodworkers throughout their entire woodworking careers, there are others who, either through volume of work or a desire to have more accurate and versatile machines, will want to invest in more professional-type equipment. Before going on to look at the range of machines available, let us first consider the conditions necessary to get the best out of them.

First and foremost, the workshop. It may be that you are thinking of using one room of the house and, if so, the two serious disadvantages are noise and vibration, particularly if the room is an upstairs one. Reducing these nuisances is not as simple as might appear, and you may need to enlist the services of a builder. But if you want to tackle the work yourself, the various Building Research Centres give advice and supply leaflets.

When thinking of the more usual outdoor workshop, it is best to accept the fact that any size much under 3m. (9ft. 9in.) × 2.5m. (8ft. lin.) is too small for anything more than a small lathe or sawbench. The ordinary single-size garage, usually about 5m. (16ft. 3in.) × 2.5m. (8ft. lin.) is, of course, a much better proposition.

Most important is the need for space to work long material. Remember that many man-made boards are at least 2.5m. (8ft. lin.) × 1.3m. (4ft. approx.), and you will appreciate how essential it is to have room for handling them. So, if the intended machine is a heavy one which cannot be moved about easily, it is vital that it is correctly sited.

For correct placing of a machine note the positions of door and window openings as it is very often possible to site the machine so that long work can be taken through either, or both, openings. The fact that timber being sawn can be cut halfway down its length, reversed, and then the other half sawn, is helpful, too. A 3m. length (9ft. approx.) would only need about half that distance—say, 2m. (6ft. approx.) at most. On the other hand, this cannot be done with an overhand planer or a thicknessing planer as in both cases the timber has to be run through its complete length in one pass.

Bear in mind too that it is often a good idea to arrange machines at different working heights so that timber being worked on one machine does not foul another. Fig. 17 gives suggested layouts.

Lighting is important, of course, and although it is pleasant to use day-light, it may be a factor which has to be sacrificed on the grounds of efficient layout. If you do have to use artificial lighting, the best arrangement is to have a source of background illumination, plus a wander lead which can be fixed temporarily to hooks in the roof or walls near each machine.

The choice of machinery is on the one hand between individual machines, each with its own function, and the universal-type machine on the other

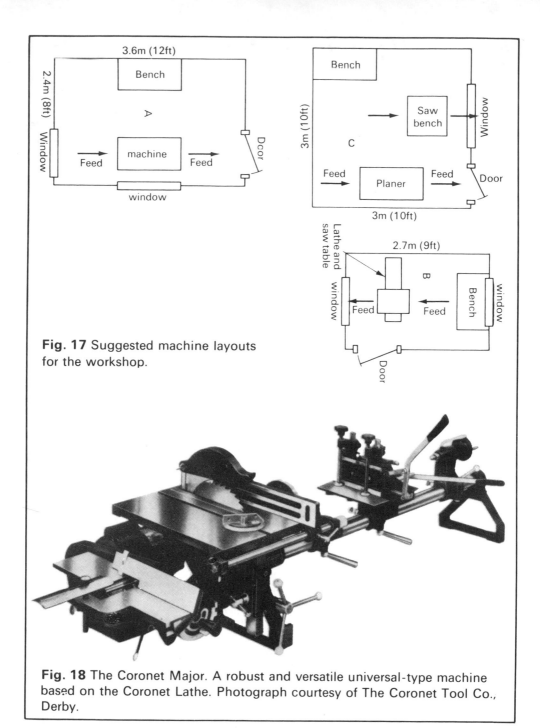

Fig. 17 Suggested machine layouts for the workshop.

Fig. 18 The Coronet Major. A robust and versatile universal-type machine based on the Coronet Lathe. Photograph courtesy of The Coronet Tool Co., Derby.

Fig. 19 The Myford saw bench attachment mounted on their ML8 lathe. Ideal for the serious amateur as it is robustly built and well-engineered. Photograph courtesy of Myfords Ltd.

comprising several attachments all working from one motor. Unless you have a really large workshop and the need for a lot of productive capacity, the universal machine is the more suitable as it is more compact and cheaper to run.

Some universal machines are based on the lathe, Fig. 18 and 19, and include attachments for planing, sawing, sanding, and mortising. Others, like that shown in Fig. 20 are basically saw benches with overhand planer and borer attachments. The one shown in Fig. 21 is unusual in that it is based on a bandsaw, with sawbench, belt sanding and disc sanding attachments, with provision for a lathe attachment and facilities for jig sawing, overhand planing, thicknessing and woodturning.

Fig. 20

Fig. 21

Fig. 20 The Minor Elliott Woodworker. Produces high-quality, professional standard work. Very suitable for those who want a degree of mass production. Photograph courtesy of Dominion Machinery Co. Ltd., Halifax.

Fig. 21 A pocket workshop on its own, the Emco Star universal woodworker. Photograph courtesy of Burgess Power Tools.

Fig. 22 A sturdy bandsaw capable of tackling most bandsawing jobs up to industrial standards. Photograph courtesy of Johnson Willow Ltd., West Molesey.

Individual machines —

Bandsaw

A bandsaw, either on its own or as an attachment, can be regarded as one of the primary machines and essential to any serious woodworking, and a typical example is shown in Fig. 22. This is interesting for its use of three wheels, not two, which gives much deeper throat clearance.

In principle, a bandsaw consists of two wheels set one above the other, the saw passing in a loop around them; a table is arranged between the wheels and the work is laid on this to be sawn. The blade is comparatively narrow—from 3mm. ($\frac{1}{8}$in.) to 6mm. ($\frac{1}{4}$in.) wide and it is possible to cut quite intricate curves and shapes as well as straight edges.

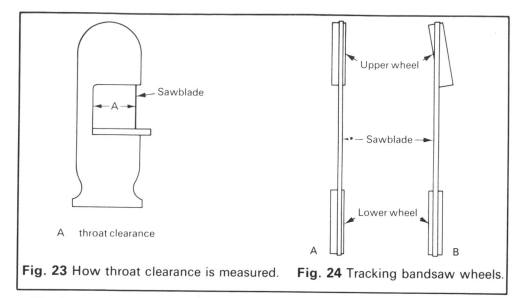

A   throat clearance

Fig. 23 How throat clearance is measured.   **Fig. 24** Tracking bandsaw wheels.

Fig. 23 shows that one of the most important factors is the throat clearance —the larger, the better. Some designs do, in fact, have three wheels so that an even larger clearance is obtained.

The lower wheel is the driver while the top one is free-running and can be moved slightly up, down, or sideways (tilted). These movements allow the saw to be put on and taken off easily and also give adjustment for tensioning. The cutting blade has a slot to allow the blade to be put on or taken off, and it can also be tilted to allow for making angled cuts. On some models a fence is fitted so that straight cuts can be made easily, cutting them free-hand is, in fact, quite difficult. However, in many cases a temporary fence can be made by cramping a spare piece of straight timber to the table to act as a guide for the work.

Cutting speed is all-important as the work should never be forced through or the saw may bend, jam, and possibly break. As a general rule the types of bandsaws being described will cut up to a 75mm. (3in.) depth of softwood but less in hardwood—perhaps only 25mm. (1in.) in a particularly dense, close-grained timber.

There are quite a lot of adjustments to be made to the saw before it can be used and once made, they should be checked frequently. First, the tension on the saw must be imposed and this is done by turning a hand wheel which raises and lowers the upper wheel. On the size of machine being considered there is unlikely to be a tension scale, so testing the tension can only be done by pressing the saw with the fingers. Too tight a saw is liable to break, while if there is too little tension there will be slack movement and a tendency for the saw to wander.

'Tracking' is another factor that needs checking from time to time. In Fig. 24A the blade is running towards the back of the wheel which is not satisfactory as it imposes uneven wear on the tyres and bearings. To correct it, turn the wheels by hand until the blade is running on the same part of both wheels. Then tilt the upper wheel slightly as at Fig. 24B so that the saw will correct its position when it has been running a little while.

The guides also need adjusting occasionally. Types of guides vary but in principle they are metal blocks which just lightly touch the saw to keep it straight. They are adjustable, and must be set back to avoid the 'set' of the saw teeth and should only just touch the saw to guide it. If they do actually rub the saw, friction and overheating can result and the temper of the steel can be affected. Incidentally, when using the bandsaw, the guides should be as near to the top of the work as is consistent with being able to follow the cutting line.

Before sawing complicated shapes, give some thought to the best way of negotiating them. It is permissible, although not desirable, to start a cut and then back the wood off, provided you keep the saw in line with the cut, and in many instances it is the only way to tackle a job. Study the examples given in Fig. 25 to get an idea of what can be done.

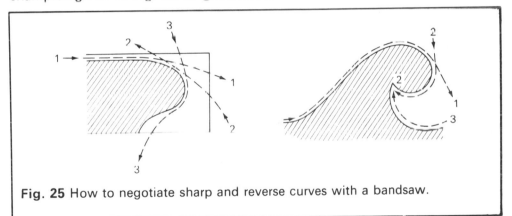

Fig. 25 How to negotiate sharp and reverse curves with a bandsaw.

Overhand planer

This is a very worthwhile machine for the woodworker who needs to be able to true-up lengths of timber quickly and without the need for constant testing with a try-square and straight-edge. A typical machine is shown in Fig. 26. It consists of a revolving drum-shaped block into which two or three knives are inserted; at one side of the drum is a 'feed' table, and at the other a 'taking-off' table.

In operation, the taking-off table (the rear table) is set to be exactly level

Fig. 26 The Coronet Overhand Planer attachment showing a pusher block

with the cutting edges of the knives, while the feed, or front table, is adjusted to the thickness of cut required, Fig. 28.

The width of the knives is, of course, a primary consideration when choosing a planer. Commercial machines can have knives up to 760mm. (30in.) or so wide, but the ones we are reviewing are more likely to range between 100mm. (4in.) and 150mm. (6in.).

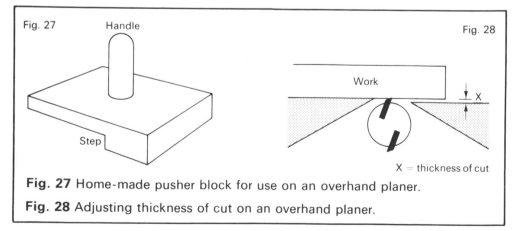

Fig. 27

Handle

Step

Fig. 28

Work

X

X = thickness of cut

Fig. 27 Home-made pusher block for use on an overhand planer.

Fig. 28 Adjusting thickness of cut on an overhand planer.

Obviously, a cutter block rotating at high speed is potentially a real danger unless treated with great respect, and all planers are fitted with adequate guards. At first sight, these guards may seem to obstruct the ability to use the machine, but if the timber is fed through properly this is not so. At no time should your hands be near the knives. To avoid this, start feeding the work from the front table with both hands, the right hand pushing it forward while the left hand holds it down on to the table. As the work gets near to the cutting knives and starts to go under the guard, the left hand is taken off the work and moved over to press down the work as it emerges on to the rear table. You can make yourself a push-block as shown in Fig. 27, which will enable you to plane small, thin stuff quite safely.

Thus, the depth of the cut is controlled by the height of the front (feed) table. This makes setting-up a straightforward business as one can rest a straight, trued-up piece of wood on the rear table so that it projects over the front table. The requisite distance can then be measured off as shown in Fig. 28, and the table height adjusted accordingly.

How much timber can be taken off at one pass is mainly a matter of experience as softwood planes much more easily than a dense hardwood. Again, a piece of hard oak will be more difficult than a piece of beech. It is probably best to set the machine to take about 2mm. ($\frac{1}{16}$in.) as an average, and let experience guide you from this!

Safety

Safety and the prevention of accidents are vital factors. It is a sad fact that some of the things that go on in a home workshop would turn a Factory Inspector's hair grey—do not think that accidents cannot happen to you.

Here is a true story to show how easily these things can catch you off-guard. The works manager of a factory where I once worked was walking round the mill one morning and stopped by a sawyer cutting some timber.

'You haven't got that machine properly guarded,' he said.

'Well,' said the sawyer, 'this is the way I always do it.'

'That's as maybe,' said the works manager, 'but you should have the guard on here,' and pointing with his finger to show where he meant, put it straight into the saw and had it cut off! And this was a man who had been dealing with woodworking machines for nearly fifty years!

The moral? Use every safety precaution that comes with the machine and *do not make any move without thinking what you are doing.* Also, do not have neckties, long sleeves or apron strings dangling, as they could get caught in moving parts with disastrous consequences. Sweep out the workshop regularly, as little wood offcuts can throw you off-balance if you step on them at the critical moment. Finally, do keep a First Aid kit in the workshop—if it does nothing else, the sight of it may help you to be careful!

Chapter 9
Working Man-made Materials

Hardboard

Unlike most other man-made boards, this material is prone to buckling after fixing if its moisture content does not match that of the surrounding atmosphere. To obviate this, the boards should be 'conditioned', which means lightly scrubbing the wrong side, i.e. the mesh side, with clean cold water. If you want to be exact, the amount of water should be 1 litre (2 pt.) per 2440mm. × 1220mm. (8ft. × 4ft.) board. After the treatment, stack the boards back-to-back and leave them for 48 hours to dry out. If you are dealing with a single board, cover the wetted side with a damp cloth to stop the moisture drying out too quickly.

There are no real difficulties in cutting hardboard provided a fine-toothed saw is used and the smooth surface kept uppermost. This ensures that any 'rag', the tiny chips and splinters which result from sawing, will occur on the back surface. Actually, if the cutting line is scored with a marking gauge or a craft knife before you start sawing, you will get an even smoother finish.

Probably the most difficult job will be arranging adequate support while you are sawing and it is worthwhile going to some trouble. Having large pieces of hardboard flapping about can damage the saw teeth, cause inaccurate sawing and result in torn edges. To prevent this you can pin or screw hardboard in place, Fig. 1A and B. There are, of course, special hardboard pins for this and they have diamond-shaped heads so that when they are hammered home the holes need no filling. But if you use standard pins then they should be punched just below the surface and the holes filled.

On standard thickness boards round- or dome-headed screws should be used. If you drive countersunk head screws right home on this type of board there is a chance that the screwholes will become so enlarged that the screws will pull through, although you could offset this by using screw cups.

Nails should be spaced about 150mm. (6in.) apart and at least 12mm. ($\frac{1}{2}$in.) from the edges to give a strong fixing which will not pull off. Also, if you are cladding a framework there is a definite sequence to follow when nailing it down, Fig. 1C. This, of course, is designed to make sure the sheet lies flat.

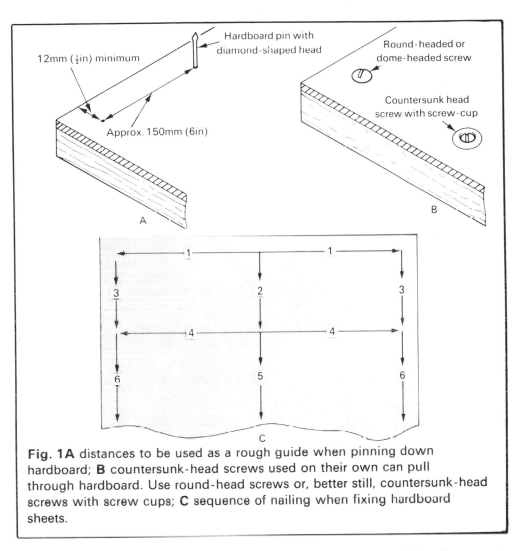

Fig. 1A distances to be used as a rough guide when pinning down hardboard; **B** countersunk-head screws used on their own can pull through hardboard. Use round-head screws or, better still, countersunk-head screws with screw cups; **C** sequence of nailing when fixing hardboard sheets.

Almost always, hardboard will be used in conjunction with a framework and a little guidance on the thicknesses of timber needed may not come amiss.

If you are building a carcase, such as a sideboard, cupboard, or wardrobe, the best size for the main framing would be 50mm. × 25mm. (2in. × 1in.), with 37mm. × 25mm. (1½in. × 1in.) for the subsidiary framings. For built-in fixtures, the main members should be 50mm. × 50mm. (2in. × 2in.). Support must be provided at intervals, too—305mm. (12in.) for 3mm. (⅛in.), 460mm. (1ft. 6in.) for 5mm. (³⁄₁₆in.), and 610mm. (2ft.) for 6mm. (¼in.) boards.

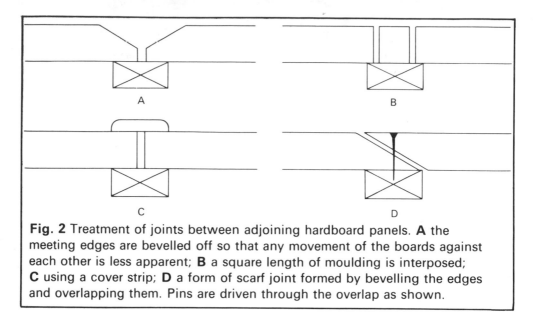

Fig. 2 Treatment of joints between adjoining hardboard panels. **A** the meeting edges are bevelled off so that any movement of the boards against each other is less apparent; **B** a square length of moulding is interposed; **C** using a cover strip; **D** a form of scarf joint formed by bevelling the edges and overlapping them. Pins are driven through the overlap as shown.

As hardboard is a comparatively thin material, jointing sheets is really a matter of butting them together and either giving a decorative appearance to the edges or masking them with some form of moulding. Fig. 2 shows some of the methods of jointing.

Hardboard can, of course, easily be bent cold along one axis—in other words, you can form a bend but you cannot bend it in a compound curve such as would be required for a dome. Depending upon the size and thickness of the piece, you should be able to bend it cold to a radius of about 762mm. (2ft. 6in.) without imposing undue strain and bursting it. One can employ

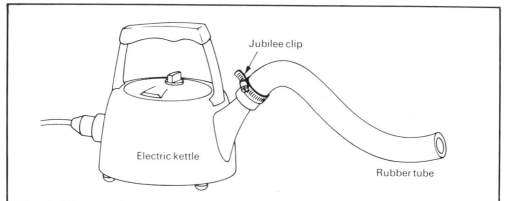

Fig. 3 Adapting an electric kettle to act as a source of steam while bending hardboard or plywood.

moderate heat to make bends of smaller radii, down to about 380mm. (1ft. 3in.). To do this, apply cloths which have been soaked in hot water and wrung out to the back (the 'mesh') side of the board and make the bend very slowly and gently, concentrating the dampening process on the part where the curve is greatest. If the piece is small enough, immerse it totally in moderately hot water doing the whole job underwater—in a bath, for instance.

Even smaller radii can be achieved by using a steaming process by which steam can be directed on to the area. Fig. 3 illustrates this with an electric kettle and a short length of rubber tubing. I prefer an electric kettle for this kind of work; if you use an ordinary kettle on a gas ring you run the risk of the excess heat setting fire to the rubber tube.

Plywood

Of all the man-made boards, plywood is the one which can be cut, sawn, or jointed in almost the same way as natural timber. One point to note, though, is that the edges of the plywood tend to wear unevenly when subjected to a sliding motion, so it is as well to avoid using plywood for sliding doors or drawer sides.

The thinnest sheets up to 2mm. ($\frac{1}{16}$in.) can best be cut with a knife and greater thicknesses with as fine-toothed a saw as possible. If you have a powered saw use a blade with as fine a tooth as possible and always arrange for the saw to feed into the show side. Ideally, a 150mm. (6in.) diameter saw is the smallest one should use to get as high a peripheral or 'tip' speed as possible. When you are sawing across the grain the face will be much less likely to splinter along the edges of the saw-cut if you score a line with a knife first.

Obviously, the thinner the plywood, the more easily it will bend but as you can see from Fig. 4A and B, it will bend more easily in one direction than in the other. It is possible to build up a bend from several separate pieces of 4mm. ($\frac{3}{16}$in.) ply (three ply) as illustrated in Fig. 4C. The thing to do is to bend the separate pieces into the shape without gluing them, using cramps as shown, and leaving them for a day. Slightly dampen the curves to help the bending, but do not attempt to glue them until they are dry and have been in the cramps.

It is perfectly feasible to form joints with multi-ply boards and, in a sense, the lapped and secret-mitre dovetail joints are particularly to be recommended as the first hides one, and the second both edges of the ply. The important factor is that the pins and tails should be about equal, as shown in Fig. 4D, page 17. Delicate, narrow pins are not practical as the ply will tend to crumble away at the necks.

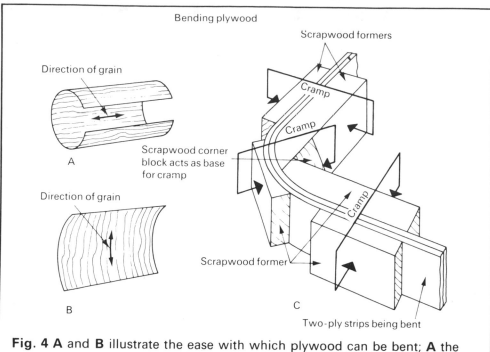

Fig. 4 A and **B** illustrate the ease with which plywood can be bent; **A** the grain of the outer plies running across the direction of bending; **B** how the opposite direction of grain can resist bending; **C** shows the set-up for a reliable way to bend plywood using scrapwood formers and blocks. Obviously, a thick bend has to be built up a few layers at a time.

Incidentally, blockboards can also be through-dovetailed or lap-dovetailed. The secret-mitre dovetail, however, would be much less effective as the blockboard core would be very liable to crumble away. If you do decide to make dovetail joints in blockboard, the same rule applies as for those in plywood—equal pins and tails; additionally, the grain of the outer veneers must run in the direction shown in Fig. 4F, page 17.

You will probably be using a cutting gauge for marking these joints out, and if so, make sure you do not sever the outer veneers otherwise they will flake off when the joint is assembled. And while talking of assembly, be sure to interpose a block of scrapwood between mallet and wood when knocking up the joints otherwise the ply will split apart.

Another corner joint which is very suitable for multi-ply boards is depicted in Fig. 4G, page 17. This is a tongued joint where a set of tongues on any board fit into corresponding slots on the other. The slots themselves are 'blind', which means that they do not penetrate the board completely and the fact that there are several of them separated by gaps of uncut wood helps to prevent crumbling of the edges. Do not forget that the slots should be made slightly oversize to accommodate the adhesive or it will all be squeezed out when the joint is assembled.

Plywood can be readily pinned or screwed and if the face is inclined to be rather soft, screw cups should be used. In any case, you will need to drill pilot holes for the screws. However, screw and nail holding abilities in the edge of plywood boards are so poor that it is better to avoid this way of fixing altogether and use an alternative.

Blockboards and chipboards

Blockboards can be cut and sawn as already described for plywood, but chipboard needs a little special treatment.

The adhesives used in making chipboard can play havoc with circular saw blades if there is a great deal to be cut, or if you are cutting it continually week after week. In this case it is advisable to invest in a TCT blade (tungsten-carbide-tipped) which will last much longer than an ordinary blade but is considerably more expensive. One fault that can occur when sawing chipboard on the circular saw is 'breaking out'. Illustrated in Fig. 5 is the fact that the saw must always project about 6mm. ($\frac{1}{4}$in.) above the chipboard surface to prevent this happening. Note, too, that the boards must always be fed into the direction of rotation. Another way to prevent spelching, (splintering of the surface when sawing) is to cover the cutting line with a strip of gummed brown paper tape. You will have to re mark the cutting line on it and then make the cut. The tape will hold the board together and prevent it crumbling; do not attempt to rip it off, but lightly soak it with water so that it peels off easily. There is, of course, no question of bending either blockboards or chipboards.

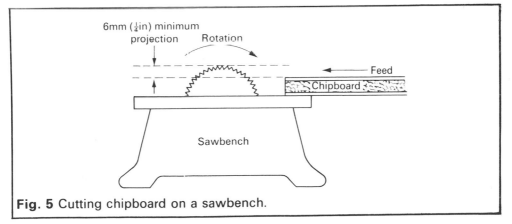

Fig. 5 Cutting chipboard on a sawbench.

Fixing in both materials present some problems. The core of blockboard is almost invariably wood of a comparatively soft nature and screw- and pin-holding abilities into either the face or the edge are bound to be weak. Consequently it is much better to rely on a substantial form of joint, plus adhesive, plus pins, or to use one or other of the special fittings shown in Chapter 11.

Chipboard also has suspect screw and nail holding powers. It is hardly worthwhile trying to pin or screw into the edges of boards as they crumble easily, but quite a good degree of holding power can be got by screwing into the face. Even so, it is much better to screw through the chipboard rather than into it as explained in Fig. 6, and it is essential to use the correct chipboard screws as shown.

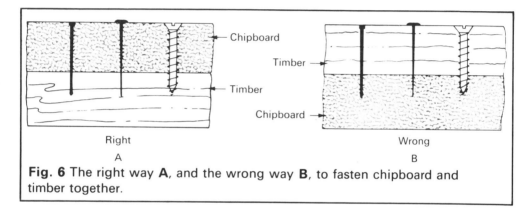

Fig. 6 The right way A, and the wrong way B, to fasten chipboard and timber together.

The various types of joints for chipboard are shown in Fig. 7 and while most are self-evident, there are some comments which may help.

In general the adhesive-only joints shown at Fig. 7A, B and C should only be used in situations where the parts will not be under stress—as infilling pieces, for instance.

The tongues in Fig. 7E and F should be in hardwood with its grain running lengthwise. Note that the grooves are made just a trifle deeper than necessary to allow space for the adhesive. Failure to do this could result in the adhesive being forced out of the joint to the detriment of the strength.

Again, the tongue in I should be hardwood. Additionally, you must be careful to allow enough thickness at the joint indicated as otherwise the board could fail.

Fig. 8 illustrates a joint which often occurs when using man-made boards as shelves and ends, and it is necessary to house one into the other. A shows the obvious way, which is to trench out the end to form a recess into which the shelf fits. This does, however, have the disadvantage that the joint will show at the front and give the job an amateurish appearance. It is much

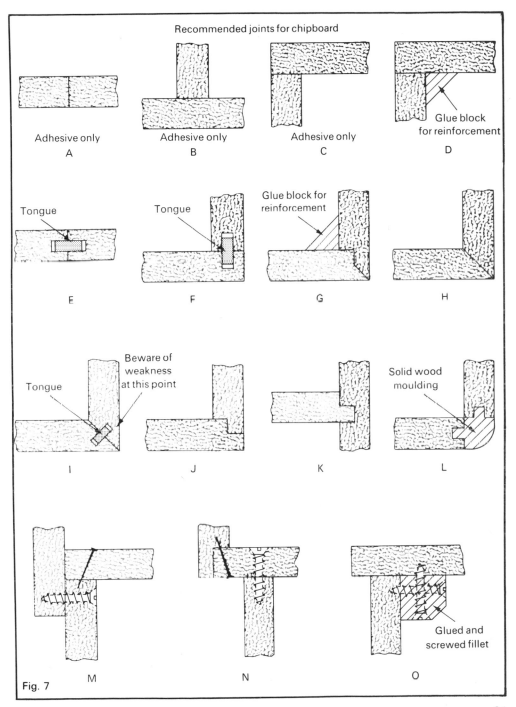

Recommended joints for chipboard

Adhesive only
A

Adhesive only
B

Adhesive only
C

Glue block
for reinforcement
D

Tongue
E

Tongue
F

Glue block for
reinforcement
G

H

Tongue
Beware of
weakness
at this point
I

J

K

Solid wood
moulding
L

M

N

Glued and
screwed fillet
O

Fig. 7

81

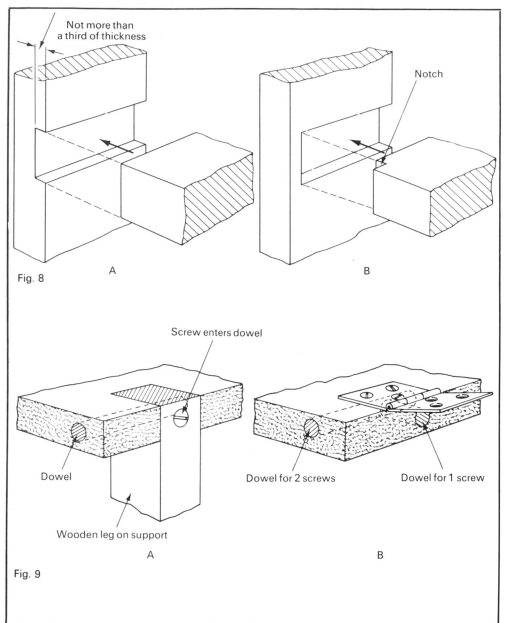

Not more than a third of thickness

Notch

Fig. 8 A B

Screw enters dowel

Dowel

Wooden leg on support

Dowel for 2 screws

Dowel for 1 screw

A B

Fig. 9

Fig. 9 How to ensure good screw holding in chipboard. **A** shows a wooden leg or support inset into a chipboard panel; a dowel is inserted as shown so that the screw penetrates it to form a really strong fixing. **B** shows the same principle applied to a hinge fixing in chipboard.

better to adopt the method shown at B, where a notch is cut from the front edge of the shelf and the trench is stopped at the front of the end.

As already mentioned, chipboard has poor nail- and screw-holding properties. There are several ways of getting over this. One way is to coat the screws with adhesive before driving them in—this is even more effective if a Rawlplug is used in conjunction with the screw. Other expedients you can adopt are shown in Fig. 9A and B. Here, ordinary hardwood dowels are used as plugs into which screws can be driven, and this is particularly useful when screwing on hinges as at B.

Plastics laminates

These can be worked with conventional woodworking tools but the fact that they are harder and more dense than plywood means that tool edges and saw teeth are blunted much more quickly. Unfortunately, it also means that unless you are careful the surface will chip, so it is imperative that all cutting tools and saws should feed into the decorative face. And, as mentioned when dealing with chipboard, a TCT saw blade is a good investment if there is a great deal of sawing to be done.

Ideally, a circular saw should be a minimum of 150mm. (6in.) diameter to achieve a high peripheral speed; you can use a portable electric saw provided the blade has fine teeth—in this case the laminate should be cut with the decorative face downwards so that the saw blade feeds into it. Plastics laminates can also be cut with a fine-toothed backsaw (a tenon saw, for instance) used at a low angle on the decorative face.

The thinner laminates such as the standard 1.5mm. ($\frac{1}{16}$in.) sheet can be cut with a Stanley knife fitted with a specially-designed, hooked blade. To do it, lay the sheet on a firm, evenly supported base such as a table or a bench with the decorative face upwards and the line to be cut as near to the table edge as possible. With the knife used against a straight edge, score the surface first lightly, then more deeply. Hold one part flat with the straight edge and pull the other part sharply upwards and the sheet should break cleanly.

Holes for screws are best made with high-speed-steel twist drills used either in a hand drill or in a machine. Always countersink the edges of such holes to avoid cracking around them.

Bending plastics laminates is not really practicable, although they can be coaxed into a gentle curve due to their innate flexibility. There is a type of laminate called 'post-formed' but this can only be bent under precise conditions of time and heat which require professional equipment.

In Figs. 10–15 you can see the sequence of operations in laying a plastics laminate down to a substrate (or base board).

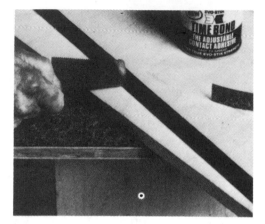
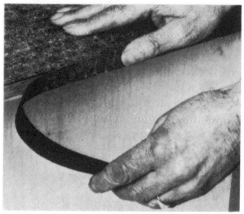

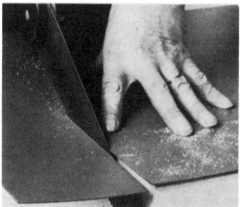

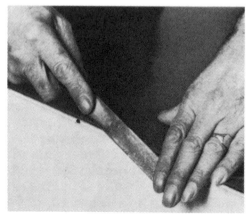

Fig. 10 (opp. top left) Using Formica Edging strip. When the first coat of adhesive applied to the edge is dry, apply a second, and also apply a coat to the edging strip. Wait for both surfaces to become dry to the touch before bringing them together. Photograph courtesy of Formica Laminate.

Fig. 11 (opp. top right) Press the strip firmly into place, but do not attempt to bend it round sharp corners. Trim the ends with scissors. Photograph courtesy of Formica Laminate.

Fig. 12 (opp. centre left) Trim the edging strip flush with a plane or upward strokes of a fine file to give a good finish. Photograph courtesy of Formica Laminate.

Fig. 13 (opp. centre right) To cover a surface with Formica Laminate, cut the panel slightly oversize with a fine-toothed saw held at a low angle, or a craft knife. During this operation, keep the decorative side of the laminate uppermost so that any small chips or splintered edges occur on the reverse side. Photograph courtesy of Formica Laminate.

Fig. 14 (opp. bottom left) Make sure the surface to which the laminate is being applied is smooth, dry and free from dust and grease. Lightly glasspaper the back of the laminate to provide a 'key' for the adhesive. Spread the adhesive in an even, thin coat on both the laminate and the surface and wait for both to become dry to the touch before bringing them together. Photograph courtesy of Formica Laminate.

Fig. 15 (opp. bottom right) After 30 minutes or so remove any overhanging edges with a flat, fine-cut file using quick downward strokes. Photograph courtesy of Formica Laminate.

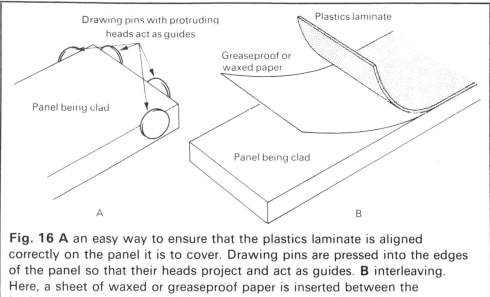

Fig. 16 A an easy way to ensure that the plastics laminate is aligned correctly on the panel it is to cover. Drawing pins are pressed into the edges of the panel so that their heads project and act as guides. B interleaving. Here, a sheet of waxed or greaseproof paper is inserted between the laminate and the panel and is withdrawn gradually as the laminate is pressed down.

1. Always cut the laminate slightly oversize all round by about 3mm. ($\frac{1}{8}$in.). This allows a margin for trimming.

2. Glasspaper both the back of the laminate and the surface to be covered to remove grease or dirt and to provide a 'key' for the adhesive.

3. Note the alternative ways of positioning the laminate, Fig. 16, so that it can be smoothed into its final position at the first attempt. Modern contact adhesives do not have the fierce grab of their predecessors so you will be able to make small adjustments before finally smoothing the laminate down.

4. A cork block, or a wooden block with a soft cloth wrapped round it makes a good 'smoother'. Work from the centre outwards to expel the air.

5. Smoothing the edges does cause some problems to some people. Use a small finely-set block plane, a cabinet scraper, or a fine-cut file, or possibly a combination of all three. Aim at finishing the edges to a steep angle of about 60 deg. to prevent them chipping.

There is a variety of edge treatments available as shown in Fig. 17. In addition, you can cut strips from the off-cuts of the laminate itself and stick them to the edges with the same adhesive and in the same manner as for the main surface. If this is done the strips should be made a trifle oversize so that you can trim them off, both top and bottom, with a fine-toothed file held at an angle of about 45 deg.

One last point to bear in mind. If the board or panel to which you are attaching the plastics laminate is unsupported by a framework, as in the case

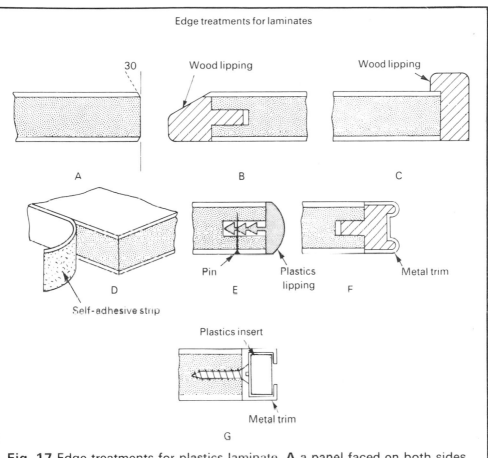

Fig. 17 Edge treatments for plastics laminate. **A** a panel faced on both sides with plastics laminate, the edges being bevelled off at an angle of about 30 deg.; **B** panel faced on the underside with a plastics laminate and its edge then grooved to accept the tongue on a solid wood moulding. Another laminate is then laid on the upper face to cover both the panel and part of the moulding, and once more the edge of the laminate is bevelled off. **C** a sound and practical way of treating the edge—the overlap of the bead effectively holds down the laminate and masks any imperfections; **D** the edge is masked with a self-adhesive veneer tape. **E**, **F**, and **G** are all proprietary edgings.

of a chipboard or blockboard door, it really is worthwhile to veneer the opposite face with a cheap backing veneer. This will prevent the board from absorbing atmospheric moisture which could cause it to warp with disastrous results to the laminate which is, of course, inert.

Storing man-made boards

Proper storing is essential and the first consideration is to keep the boards as dry as possible. The best way to ensure this is shown in Fig. 18A where 75mm. × 50mm. (3in. × 2in.) bearers are spaced at 406mm.–500mm. (1ft. 4in.–1ft. 7¾in.) intervals. Note too, that the top bearers which support some suitable kind of protective material are placed in positions which correspond to those of the bearers on the floor. The protective material should preferably be fairly weighty to prevent the top board warping. However, if this should happen, turning the board over usually remedies it.

But it is very likely that you do not have many flat spaces 2440mm. × 1220mm. (8ft. × 4ft.) going free in your home for months at a time!

What most of us have to settle for is the workshop or, more likely, the garage, and this means leaning the boards against a wall, as in Fig. 18B, but you must take one or two precautions. Firstly, do not let the bottom edges of the boards rest on the floor or any damp or condensation could migrate into the edges and buckle them. Rest them on the type of bearers already discussed. Secondly, do not allow them to lean against the wall with no means of support or they will surely buckle. Provide bearers at the correct distances for them to lean against and take care that these bearers all lean at the same angle.

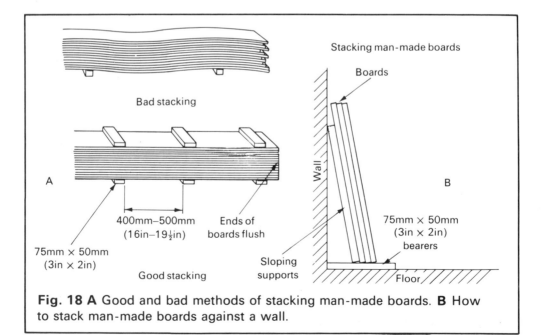

Fig. 18 A Good and bad methods of stacking man-made boards. **B** How to stack man-made boards against a wall.

Chapter 10
Modern Upholstery Techniques and Materials

It would be an over-statement to say that the old-time upholsterer worked in a constant state of frustration, but in my mind are memories of many hours spent trying to design a frame which, when upholstered, would have the rounded, sculptured and comfortable appearance of the present-day settee.

The trouble was that it entailed making up the basic frame and adding blocks and rails which, when upholstered, would approximate to the desired shape. Chapter 2, Fig. 9 shows what I mean. Even though it is a comparatively straightforward design, the basic frame has had extra blocks fixed on the arms, at the top of the back, and on the front rail. Add to this the spring-units for the seat, the back, and the arms and the whole thing begins to get a trifle complicated!

Industrial chemistry has, however, come to the rescue and by introducing plastic and latex foams has enabled people like us to undertake what would otherwise be some very formidable upholstery.

Figs. 1 and 2, and also Chapter 12, Fig. 7 show various ways of providing platforms or supports for loose cushions. Generally, the method of springing is the same for the seat and the back for any particular chair. For a tension-sprung seat you would normally use a tension-sprung back, with a rubber-webbed seat, a rubber-webbed back, but there is no reason why you should not mix the methods. In fact, in Chapter 12, Fig. 7 you can see that while the seat uses tension springs, the back uses Pirelli webbing.

Reverting to Fig. 1, the tension springs shown are sold in several lengths to suit various seat or back widths: allow about 38mm.–50mm. (1½in.–2in.) for tensioning, so if you have to span a 460mm. (1ft. 6in.) seat width, use a 406mm. (1ft. 4in.) spring. When they were first introduced, such springs were supplied in the bare steel which had to be covered with a cloth to protect the cushion from being soiled. Today, however, they are invariably covered with individual plastic sleeves.

The method shown in Fig. 1A involves anchoring the springs through holes in a metal strip which is nailed or screwed to the seat rail. Note that the strip is rebated into the rail so that neither the heads of the fixing screws nor the edges of the metal strip itself can protrude and tear the cushion cover.

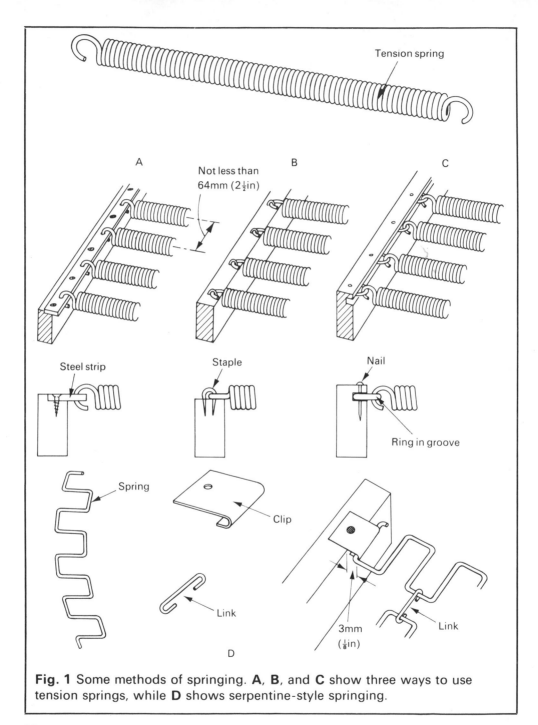

Fig. 1 Some methods of springing. **A**, **B**, and **C** show three ways to use tension springs, while **D** shows serpentine-style springing.

By the same token, the 'hook' formed by pulling out the last coil of the spring must always point downwards so that it cannot snag the cushion.

Stapling, as at B, is another method which is quite often used. Admittedly, it is easy and cheap but that is about all there is to recommend it. The disadvantages are that there is a tendency for the sideways tension on the staple to split the edge of the wood away. Further, as the hook must necessarily lie flat there is a likelihood that its sharp point could snag the cushion cover.

The method shown at C is undoubtedly the neatest and most effective way of solving the problem. As you can see, the 'works' are hidden and all that is visible is a neat row of nail heads (use round-headed nails), and there is no grinding noise such as occurs with method A when the cushion is sat on.

From the illustration you will gather that a groove has to be cut near the top edge of the seat rail, and this is usually about 10mm ($\frac{3}{8}$in.) deep by 3mm. ($\frac{1}{8}$in.) wide. The groove is cut to accept rings into which the hooks of the springs are anchored, and suitable rings are supplied with the springs. Do not be tempted to use other kinds of rings as they are invariably too weak and distort in shape when tension is continually placed on them.

The 'serpentine' style springing illustrated at D is also widely used and is particularly suitable for springing small (dining chair) seats. Each length is in the form of a flattened curve, and it is this curvature combined with the springiness of the metal which creates the resiliency. Fixing is simplicity itself, as the illustration shows.

Pirelli rubber webbing, Fig. 2, makes a perfect platform for loose cushions as it is clean, neat, straightforward to fix, and noiseless in operation.

As shown at A the webbing is available in four widths: 18mm. ($\frac{3}{4}$in.); 28mm. ($1\frac{1}{8}$in.); 37mm. ($1\frac{1}{2}$in.); and 50mm. (2in.). What width you employ depends, of course, on for what and how the webbing is being used. Thus, the thinnest webbing in single strand form would be suitable for dining chair seats or small stools; however, interlace it in a criss-cross fashion and it could be used in a fireside or occasional chair. The most popular width is the 28mm. ($1\frac{1}{8}$in.) one, followed by the 50mm. (2in.) width for large, heavy designs such as beds.

The method of tacking is important as wrongly placed tacks can weaken the fixing and could eventually cause the webbing to split round the tack holes. For this reason, the numbers of tacks used and their positioning are shown at A. There is another point to bear in mind: when tacking, always allow about 25mm. (1in.) surplus on the end which is being tacked down as this will go a long way to avoiding the likelihood of splits.

One more feature to remember is shown at B where the edge of the rail is rounded off to avoid the webbing being continually chafed by a sharp edge.

Fig. 2C illustrates the professional way of anchoring the webbing, and

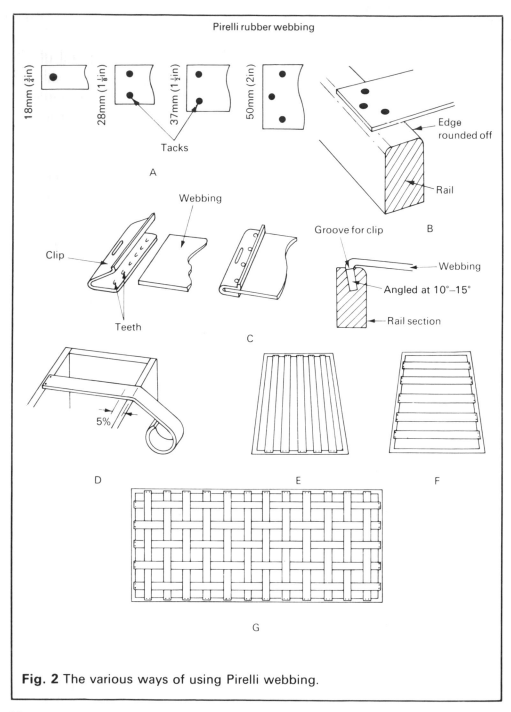

Fig. 2 The various ways of using Pirelli webbing.

it is certainly preferable to tacking. A small-toothed clip is used which is supplied with the webbing. It is positioned over the end of the webbing and clamped up to grip firmly—an ordinary bench vice will do this perfectly.

A groove has to be cut to accept the clips and details are shown at C. The most important point is that the groove has to be cut at a slight angle of 10 deg.–15 deg. so that it is opposed to the pulling effort of the webbing. The groove size is 12mm. ($\frac{1}{2}$in.) deep by 7mm. ($\frac{5}{32}$in.) wide.

The degree of tension should be a minimum of 5% of the untensioned length, in other words 25mm. in 500mm. (1in. in 20in.) and so on, but for most purposes this could well be increased to $7\frac{1}{2}$%.

Webbing patterns for chairs depend on the design of the chair seat. At E the seat tapers and the webbing strands are arranged to follow the taper. Bear in mind the general rule that the spaces between individual strands should not be greater than the widths of the strands themselves, or not appreciably so. Fig. 2F gives an interesting variation for the tapered seat problem, and this method is probably stronger as the strands are closer together at the back (narrow) end of the seat which is where there is the greatest imposed weight. A typical arrangement of strands for a single size divan bed is shown at G. The total pull of the strands imposes a great strain on the long sides of the frame and therefore it is advisable to build in a cross strut halfway along the length to give added strength.

Plastics foam

This derives from the petro-chemical industry and is, in fact, polyether. Polyester, another by-product of the same industry, is also used in upholstery but only for fabric-laminated covering material.

It is not within the scope of this book to go into the methods of producing polyether foam as our concern is solely with the foam as a finished product.

Besides the foam itself, there is another upholstery material derived from it called 'chipfoam'. This is made by chipping or granulating standard polyether foam and embedding the chips in a liquid form of the original foam. Under compression the mixture hardens to densities which can be up to ten times greater than the standard foam, although they can be cut in exactly the same way.

Returning to the standard polyether foam, let us compare its resiliency with that of latex foam. The latter has the characteristics of compressing at an even rate so that if you sit on a cushion of latex foam you will sink down gradually and evenly.

Polyether foam, on the other hand, has the characteristic that, although the initial resistance to compression is high, once a certain point is reached the resistance suddenly decreases giving the sitter a sharp descent! This feature is not as bad as it used to be since the foam structure has been modified to eliminate it as far as possible.

The reason for the difference between the resiliency characteristics of latex and polyether foams lies in the fact that the hardness or softness of latex is in direct ratio to its density (expressed in weight per cubic foot), but in polyether the chemical structure can be formulated to incorporate a separate hardness characteristic quite irrespective of its density. Thus, while a firm latex foam has a high latex to air ratio, a soft latex will have a low latex to air ratio. On the other hand, a firm polyether foam can have either a high or low density.

Obviously, this question of densities and hardnesses is a prime factor when buying polyether foam. The foam is made in the following densities: 1 lb. to 1.5 lb. per cubic foot for light upholstery use such as head rests, arm pads, back cushions; 1.5 lb to 1.8 lb per cubic foot for seats on small chairs, back cushions, arms, mattresses; 1.8 lb. to 3 lb. per cubic foot for seat cushions—the higher densities should be used for seat and back cushions where they will receive hard wear—seating in public halls, for instance.

The hardness factor is up to the individual, but as a pointer remember that a low density/high hardness foam will soon deteriorate in hard service. So the rule for hardness is the same as for density—the higher the hardness, the better it will withstand wear.

Another option concerns the thickness of the foam, bearing in mind that you can laminate or build up slabs of different densities, and that the kind of base used will also govern the best type of foam to use. The simplest base is obviously a straightforward wooden one, and here the foam alone produces all the softness and resilience. So, a firm grade for seating purposes would need to be at least 89mm. (3½in.) thick, or a softer grade a thickness of at least 114mm. (4½in.). In this context, hessian webbing, wooden slatted bases, and glassfibre shells should be classed as solid bases.

However, in many cases, easy-chairs and possibly the backs as well, are ready-sprung with tension springs, rubber elastic webbing, or serpentine springing. This means that the thicknesses can be reduced so that the firmer grade need only be 75mm. (3in.) thick, and the softer grade 100mm. (4in.) thick.

There is a drawback here that you must watch for, and that is that the frame rails may be in contact with the cushion when the seat is occupied, which can be uncomfortable and irksome for the occupant. It will mean either padding the rail, or moving it so that contact does not occur.

It may well be that a 100mm. (4in.) cushion will look ungainly in a particular chair, or it may be impossible to have such a thickness because the design precludes it—this might well occur if you are making a convertible settee. The problem can be overcome by sticking slabs of different hardnesses together. In this way, a 100mm. (4in.) cushion could be reduced to 75mm. (3in.) by joining together one 50mm. (2in.) soft grade slab to one 25mm. (1in.) firmer grade.

In addition to the slab form or sheet form of polyether foam, there is a derivative called 'profile-cut' foam. It is made by feeding a slab of standard foam through a machine containing special projecting hammers; the effect of the operation is to split the slab into halves. Each half has one face which is the normal smoothness, but the reverse face has a contoured shape giving the egg-box effect shown in Fig. 3.

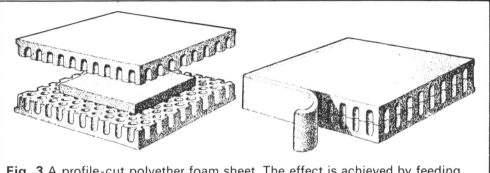

Fig. 3 A profile-cut polyether foam sheet. The effect is achieved by feeding a slab of the foam through rollers covered with projecting adjustable hammers which distort the foam as a knife passes through the centre. On recovery from this process the cut surfaces have a contoured shape.

Figs. 3, 5 and **6** appear by kind permission of the British Rubber Manufacturers Association Ltd. from whose booklet *Latex Foam Handbook* by Dennis Young, pages 3, 4, 5, 6, these diagrams were taken.

The resulting pieces have a delicately soft feel and typical uses are for pillows and cushions where a piece of standard slab foam is sandwiched between two pieces of profile-cut foam to achieve the conventional shape.

Working polyether foam

Cutting the foam neatly can be tricky, particularly when it is in the greater thicknesses. If you have an electric carving knife you will find it ideal for the job; alternatives are a long and thin chef's knife which must be razor sharp, or a fine-toothed hacksaw blade.

A ballpoint pen or tailor's chalk can be used for marking out. Always cut the foam oversize and the covers to the exact finished dimensions as this will ensure that when the foam is in its fabric cover it will be under slight tension. This, of course, will ensure that there are no wrinkles in the cover. As a rough guide, cut a mattress about 20mm. ($\frac{3}{4}$in.) oversize all round, and a chair seat or back cushion about 12mm. ($\frac{1}{2}$in.).

If the covering material does not breathe air freely, you will either have to sew in ventilation eyelets, or make one side from an open-weave cloth. If this is not done, air cannot escape when the foam is compressed.

Fig. 4 shows you how to bevel edges, cut shapes, make domed shapes and do buttoning. At A the edge of a bench or table and a steel straight-

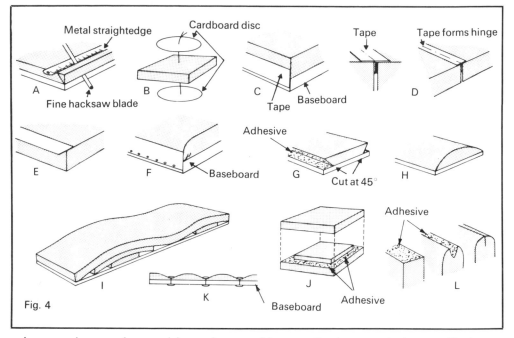

Fig. 4

edge can be used as guides when making vertical or angled cuts. B shows how, to cut a circle or other curved shapes, two templates of hardboard or stiff cardboard are needed. The foam is sandwiched between them and the whole assembly is secured with a length of wire prior to cutting round it. C illustrates cushions fixed permanently to a solid base by applying a 75mm. (3in.) band of adhesive around the edges. If you want to be able to remove the cushion at any time, glue tape to the edges and then tack it to the base. The completed assembly ready for the fabric covering is shown at C. D shows how to form hinges when, for instance, seat and back cushions have to be joined; E the tape stuck to the foam, and F how it forms a rounded edge when taken over and tacked to the base.

Padded backs and seats are shown in G, H, and I. Chamfer the edges of the foam and glue them to the base as at G to form the shape shown in H. Gluing small pads to a baseboard and overlaying them with a larger slab will enable you to achieve the shape shown at I. To make a domed shape for a cushion, use the method shown at J where two slabs have a smaller piece sandwiched between them. The larger slabs are, of course, each half the finished thickness of the cushion, while the small pad is about 75mm. (3in.) smaller all round and about 25mm. (1in.) thick.

To fix buttons in cushions or chair backs use a 25mm. (1in.) thick layer of soft foam over a slab of a firmer grade and fix the buttons through both, K. For a bed head stick a 38mm. (1½in.) layer of soft grade foam to the hard-board or plywood back and button through. L shows a neat and simple way to form rounded edges. Apply adhesive to the edge of the cushion, allow it to become tacky and then pinch the edges together.

Chipfoam

This is available in various thicknesses from 2mm. ($\frac{1}{12}$in.) upwards and is particularly useful as a base sheet on to which softer foam can be stuck. Alternatively, it can be used in conjunction with a rubber profile (Fig. 4) to create a sculptured appearance.

Latex foam

The first latex foams were made of the natural latex from the rubber tree but modern ones are from man-made styrene-butadiene latex, or from a blend of the two. Foaming can be effected either by mechanically forcing air into the latex or induced by stirring in hydrogen peroxide and a catalyst.

As we have seen, the resilience of latex foam is governed by one factor only, the latex to air ratio, and unlike polyether foam there is no hardness factor. This means that there are fewer grades and in fact there are seven, ranging from Super Soft for pillows and scatter cushions, to Extra Firm for use with rigid bases and in conditions of heavy wear.

Fig. 5 shows the types of latex foam available. A is a non-reversible unit. This has a smooth top surface while the underside shows the cavities pro-duced during moulding. There is a wide range of sizes, shapes, and grades of firmness. A reversible unit is shown at B. This is made from two non-reversible units glued together, cavity side to cavity side. Again, there is a wide range of sizes, shapes and grades of firmness; this is, in fact, the standard pattern for loose cushions for three-piece suites and fireside chairs. C is cavity sheet which has a smooth top surface, while the underside shows the cavities. It is mainly used for hand building, and can be had in many sheet sizes and thicknesses. D is plain sheet used in hand building and for such things as dining chair seats and backs. Again, available in many sheet

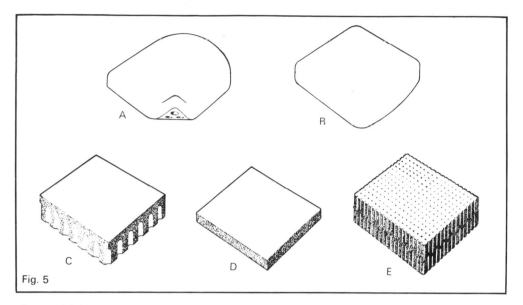

Fig. 5

sizes, thicknesses and degrees of firmness. E illustrates pincore block—a brilliant idea, whereby the block has pin holes formed on opposing sides with the result that all surfaces present a uniform smoothness. It is ideal for mattresses and pillows, and cushions made from it require no sidewalling.

Working latex foam

Working methods are very similar to those employed with plastics foam. Tailor's chalk or a ballpoint pen will give good marking lines and a pair of really sharp, large scissors or a sharp knife will do the cutting. Wetting the cutting edges with cold water will make the job easier as water is a natural lubricant for rubber.

As with plastic foam, latex should be cut slightly oversize, allowing about 5mm. ($\frac{3}{16}$in.) on every 250mm. (10in.). The cover itself should be cut to exact size so that when the oversize foam is inserted there will be no wrinkling. Regarding ventilation, the remarks apply as for polyether foam.

Fig. 6 shows the various finishes for latex foam. A illustrates a square edge. First apply 12mm. ($\frac{1}{2}$in.) plain sheet strips to the outside of a piece of cavity sheet foam to form walls—a process known as 'sidewalling'. When finished, the unit should be very slightly larger than the base to which it is to be attached. The tape is stuck to the vertical edge of the foam and is shown with an overhang which is tacked to the base. B shows a feathered edge. Here the cavity sheet foam is cut to finish about 12mm. ($\frac{1}{2}$in.) larger all round than the base to which it is to be fixed—this cut is a vertical one. Next,

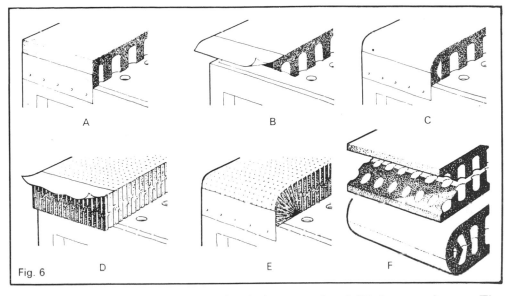

Fig. 6

cut the edges so that they taper back at an angle of 45 deg. as shown. The tape is stuck to the edge and then pulled down and tacked to the base with tacks spaced about 75mm. (3in.) apart. The cushioned edge is illustrated at D. The procedure is the same as for the feathered edge, except that the sides are not cut but left vertical. The advantage of this method is that the edge has a firmer feel due to the fact that none has been cut away. F shows feather-edge cushions. Two pieces of cavity sheet latex foam are needed for this. Both should be the same thickness. Taper back the sides as shown, bearing in mind that the degree of taper determines the radius of the finished edge. Spread a thin layer of adhesive on to each tapered edge and allow it to become tacky before pressing them together firmly.

With all types of edge finish, the latex foam is held in position on the base by means of taping. Cotton tape, or strips of calico 50mm. (2in.) or 64mm. ($2\frac{1}{2}$in.) wide are used. Adhesive should be spread thinly along half the width of the tape and in a similar width on to the latex foam. Allow the adhesive to become tacky and then press the tape firmly on to the latex foam and dust with French chalk to avoid stickiness. The free edge of the tape can then be stuck, tacked, or stapled to the base.

Where solid wooden bases are used in conjunction with latex or polyether foam mattresses, adequate ventilation holes must be provided. The recommended requirements are for 20mm. ($\frac{3}{4}$in.) diameter holes at 100mm. (4in.) centres. It is better not to lay a foam mattress directly on to an open wire mesh base, but to interpose a reasonably taut underlay.

Chapter 11
Hinges, Knock-down and Other Fittings

The difficulties of making quick and easy joints in man-made boards, plus the need to cut down time spent on assembly in the factory, have led to the development of a wide array of fittings and hinges.

Some of these are called KD ('Knock-Down') fittings as they enable the furniture to be packed flat for transportation and assembled by unskilled labour at its destination, whether it be a shop or a private customer.

The diagrams show a representative selection to cover most of the fixing and hingeing problems you are likely to meet.

Fig. 1 Two types of tee-nuts. **A** shows the pronged type which can be driven into the wood. **B** illustrates the round-base screw-on type. Both accept metal threaded bolts or studding and are made in several diameters.

Fig. 2 A plastic barbed dowel, 5.5mm. diameter ($\frac{3}{16}$in.) by 30mm. long ($1\frac{3}{16}$in.). The dowel is knocked into the hole on one member and then the adjacent piece is knocked on to the part which protrudes; the barbs hold the dowel firmly into the holes.

Fig. 3 Cylindrical hinge which is suitable for hingeing lay-on or inset doors. **A** identical holes have to be bored on both the door and the side and the opening angle is 180 deg. Made in three sizes—10mm. ($\frac{3}{8}$in. full), 15mm. ($\frac{9}{16}$in.), and 16mm. ($\frac{5}{8}$in.).

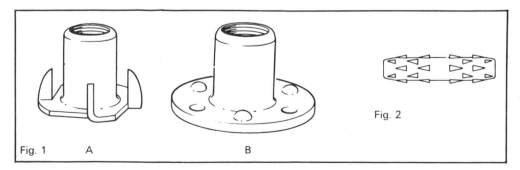

Fig. 1   A   B   Fig. 2

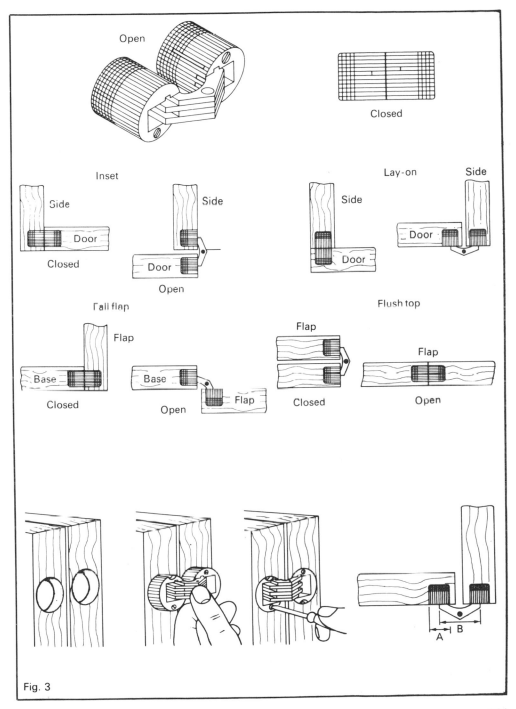

Open

Closed

Inset

Side

Side

Door

Closed

Door

Open

Lay-on

Side

Side

Side

Door

Door

Fall flap

Flap

Flap

Base

Base

Flap

Closed

Open

Flush top

Flap

Flap

Closed

Open

A   B

Fig. 3

101

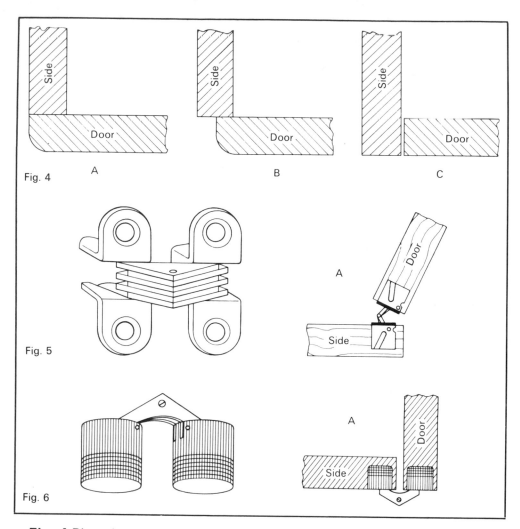

Fig. 4 Plan views showing the difference between lay-on and inset doors. **A** and **B** show two kinds of lay-on doors where the door either partly or wholly laps over the side of the carcase; **C** shows an inset door which is enclosed by the carcase side.

Fig. 5 Concealed hinge for lay-on or inset doors. It is recessed into mortises on both the door and the side, and it is made for doors 18mm. ($\frac{3}{4}$in.) thick.

Fig. 6 Cylindrical type of concealed hinge for lay-on or inset doors. It fits into holes bored in the door and the side as at **A**. It is made in sizes from 15mm. ($\frac{9}{16}$in.) to 25mm. (1in.) thicknesses of timber.

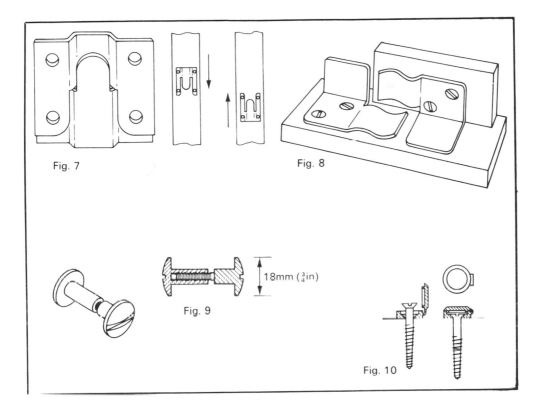

Fig. 7

Fig. 8

18mm (¾in)

Fig. 9

Fig. 10

Fig. 7 The 'Flushmount' fitting acts on the principle of two steel tongues interlocking and can be used wherever two flat, parallel surfaces need to be joined. Examples are fixing lightweight cabinets to each other or to walls, or in carcase construction generally where the adjacent members are of suitable thickness.

Fig. 8 Interlocking right-angle fitting. This works on the principle of two interlocking steel tongues, and is specifically for use where sides meet at right angles.

Fig. 9 A cabinet-connecting screw which comprises two plastic caps screwed on to a metal studding. A very simple device, it is often used for joining kitchen units. All that is needed is to bore a matching hole in both units, insert the studding and tighten up the caps with a screwdriver.

Fig. 10 A polythene screw-cover cap. This is an alternative to the well-known screw-cup. Particularly good on screws which pass through thin material where traditional countersinking could be a weakness.

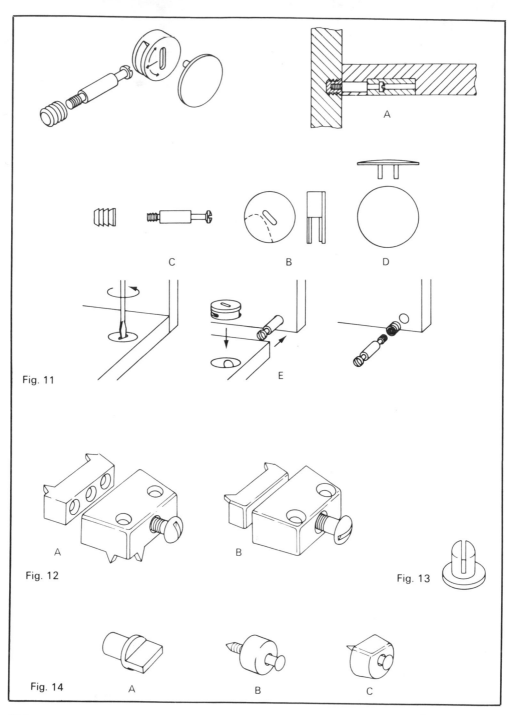

Fig. 11

Fig. 12

Fig. 13

Fig. 14

Fig. 11 The 'Fix' cam fitting is generally useful for cabinet construction, particularly when chipboard is used, although the material must be 13mm. ($\frac{1}{2}$in.) thick or more. The cam can be tightened by turning a screwdriver in the slot when the cam bears on the bolt and takes up any slack between the parts being joined. Finally, a plastic cap can be pressed into the cam to hide the parts.

Diagrams **A, B, C, D,** and **E** show details of fixing. The nylon bush can be merely pushed into its hole, but its holding power is improved by using a PVA adhesive as well.

Fig. 12 Two corner jointing blocks. **A** is the pattern where both parts have prongs so that they can be tapped into position; in **B** only one part is pronged.

Fig. 13 A neat plastic guide to enable drawers to slide easily. Two are fitted to the bottom of the drawer at the back, and one at each end of the carcase rail at the front. Size of hole required is 5mm. ($\frac{3}{16}$in.) diameter, and the guides are press-fit.

Fig. 14 Three types of plastic shelf stud. **A** is simply tapped into a hole, while **B** and **C** are both pinned in place.

Fig. 15 Self-explanatory.

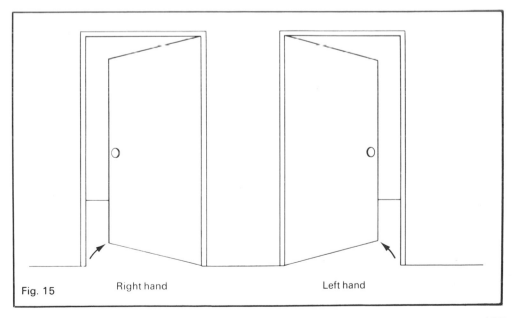

Fig. 15   Right hand   Left hand

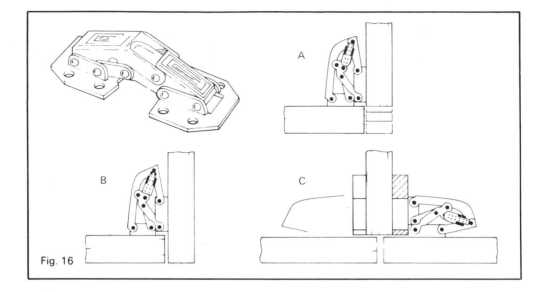

Fig. 16

Fig. 16 A surface-fixing invisible hinge which is completely concealed when the doors are closed. No machining or recessing is required as the hinge is merely screwed on. For lay-on doors, and for two doors hung to a common stile **C**.

Fig. 17 A corner-jointing block called by several proprietary names. It is made in strong plastic and comprises two parts, one containing a locking nut and the other two recesses for the pegs. The latter part also houses a locking screw. The parts are screwed to those being joined as at **B**, and the locking screw is driven home into the locking nut once the pegs have been located into their holes.

Fig. 18 Steel corner bracket.

Fig. 19 A form of metal dowel fitting which gives a very strong joint. It consists of a 6mm. ($\frac{1}{4}$in.) diameter steel bolt which penetrates a metal cross-dowel, a collar being supplied to house the countersunk head.

Fig. 20 A pivot hinge for use with lay-on rebated doors; it has threaded arms which screw into 5mm. ($\frac{3}{16}$in.) diameter holes. The hinge itself is electro-brassed and polished, and as it is mounted on the outside it forms a decorative feature. On chipboard doors it is advisable to sink a nylon plug into the edge into which you can screw the hinge arm.

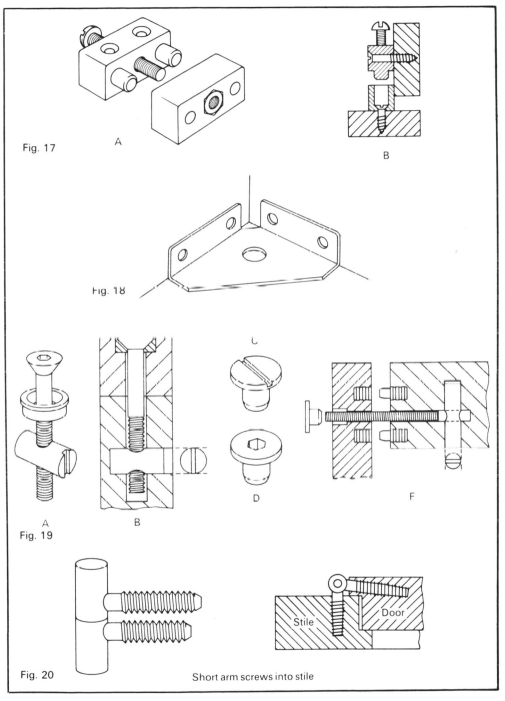

Fig. 17

A

B

Fig. 18

Fig. 19

A

B

C

D

F

Fig. 20

Short arm screws into stile

Stile

Door

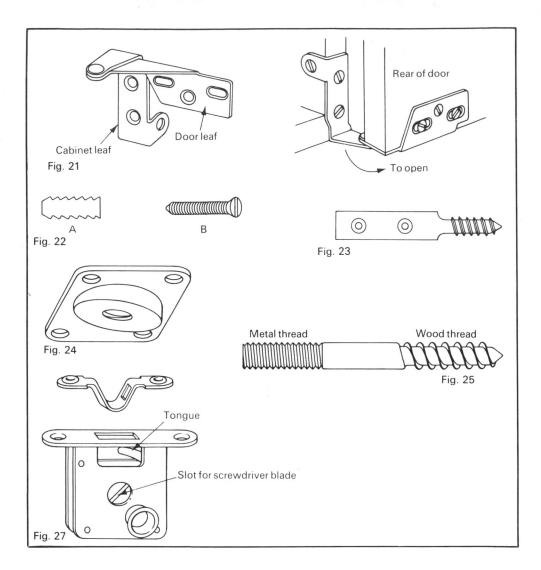

Fig. 21

Cabinet leaf

Door leaf

Rear of door

To open

Fig. 22

A

B

Fig. 23

Fig. 24

Metal thread

Wood thread

Fig. 25

Tongue

Slot for screwdriver blade

Fig. 27

Fig. 21 Another pivot hinge for lay-on doors. They come in handed pairs as one is fitted to the top of the door and the other to the bottom. The big advantage is that no cutting in or recessing is needed as the hinges are simply screwed in place; another good point is that they allow a 180 deg. opening.

Fig. 22 Fasteners for chipboard. **A** is a nylon bush which is glued into a 8mm. ($\frac{5}{16}$in.) diameter hole; **B** is the appropriate screw which is driven into it.

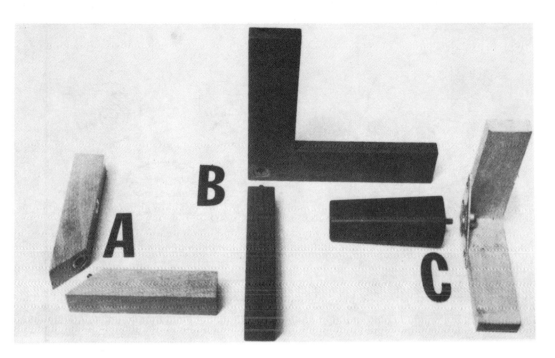

Fig. 23 Stretcher plate.

Fig. 24 Table leg plate. This is screwed to the underside of a table top; the central hole is tapped to accept a metal pin which is inserted in the end of the leg.

Fig. 25 Dowel screw with part threaded for use in wood, and part for metal.

Fig. 26 (above) The 'Kea' range of joint fittings. **A** shows the mitred joint assembly. **B** is the standard joint for legs; **C** illustrates a special leg fitting mounted on a triangular metal plate.
The fitting consists of a 22mm. ($\frac{7}{8}$in.) sleeve threaded externally for wood or metal or a combination of both, with two hardened cup springs and a threaded nut set in a cylindrical recess and hexagonal aperture. The final 360 deg. turn is under tension and allows the leg to be positioned correctly. Once fixed, the leg will not vibrate loose and will remain under tension if the timber dries out. Marketed in U.K. by Scantact Ltd., Greenford, Middx.

Fig. 27 Mortise-type KD fitting for joining panels end-to-end. The tongue is moved over to lock the fitting by inserting a screwdriver blade in the slot and turning it.

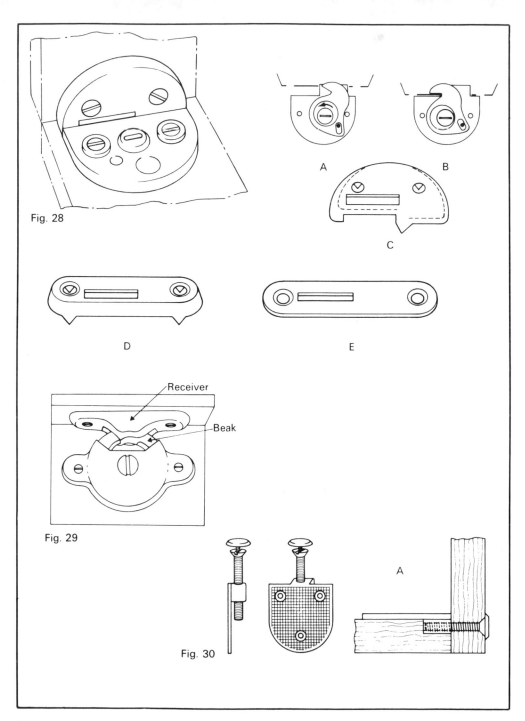

Fig. 28

A

B

C

D

E

Receiver

Beak

Fig. 29

Fig. 30

A

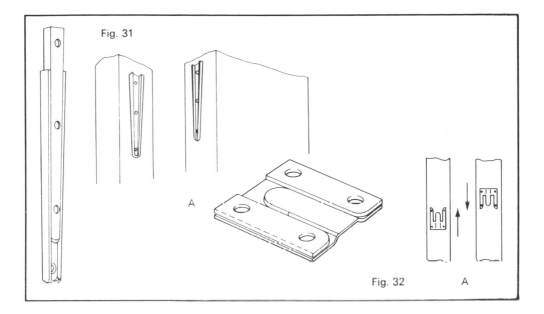

Fig. 31

Fig. 32   A

Fig. 28 Another KD fitting for joining panels at right angles, particularly suited to large pieces of furniture such as wardrobes. **A** shows how the locating tongue enters the receiver plate; **B** how the 'beak' locks by being turned by the movement of the central cam; **C** is a two-way receiver plate; **D** a raised receiver plate, and **E** a flat receiver plate. An ordinary screwdriver blade fits the slot in the cam for turning it.

Fig. 29 A fitting similar to the one in **Fig. 28** which joins panels at right angles. The beak is a tapered one which exerts considerable tightening power as it moves into the receiver.

Fig. 30 Another method of fixing panels at right angles. However, it is not as strong as either **Fig. 28** or **Fig. 29**. The principle involved is self-evident; note the detachable cap which conceals the screw head.

Fig. 31 This is a tapered connector for joints which are required to be invisible—boards butted edge-to-edge, for example, or (in upholstered work) joining arms to backs after upholstery.

Fig. 32 A flush mount. This is for mounting objects flush by means of the mating tongues. Typical uses are for mounting cabinets on walls, or for joining panels.

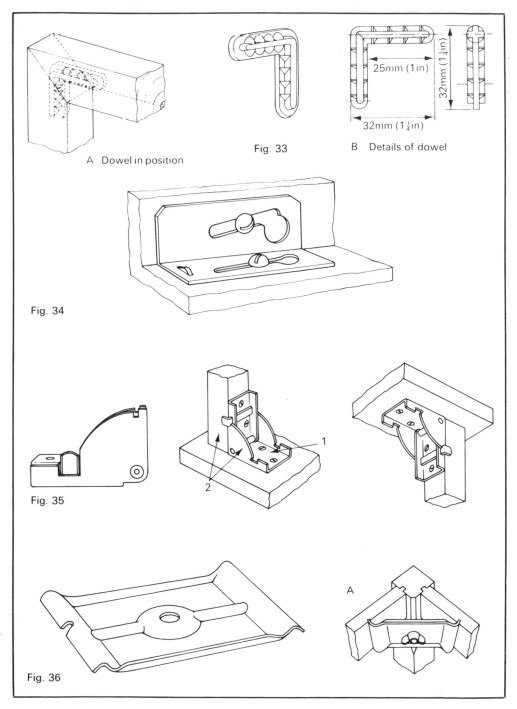

A   Dowel in position

Fig. 33

B   Details of dowel

25mm (1in)

32mm (1¼in)

32mm (1¼in)

Fig. 34

Fig. 35

1

2

Fig. 36

A

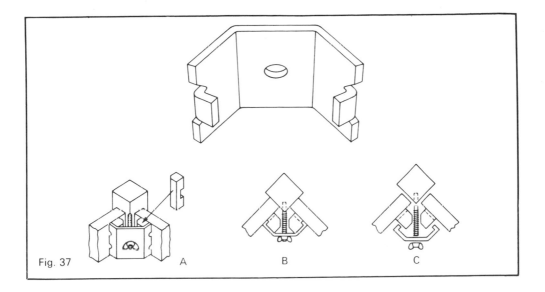

Fig. 37   A   B   C

Fig. 33 Plastic mitre dowels. You will need to bore the holes for these first before cutting the mitre, and a gap-filling adhesive should be used.

Fig. 34 Angled connector plate, left or right hand. Useful for strengthening panels meeting at right angles, particularly when they require to be dismantled frequently. To do this, merely unscrew the screw head a turn or two and the plate can be slid free.

Fig. 35 Bracket for folding legs on tables. This has a very strong and positive action with a self-locking device. **A** to fix, lay the table top on a flat, firm surface with the underside facing upwards. Open the bracket, set the side without the spring in position and insert three screws. **B**, fasten the leg to the rear side of the spring locking section with three screws, holding the leg down flush with the table top throughout the procedure.

Fig. 36 The table brace plate, an extremely useful device. This is an efficient means of reinforcing the corner of a frame, particularly of a chair or table, and is used in conjunction with a dowel screw (see **Fig. 25**).
The lugs on the edges of the plate are located in grooves cut in the rails as at **A** and the dowel screw is inserted into the corner of the leg via a pre-bored hole.

Fig. 37 KD table plate. Similar to **Fig. 36**, but the lugs locate into grooves cut in the blocks shown at **A** and **B**. Releasing the wing nut allows the lugs to be withdrawn **C**, and the fitting can be dismantled.

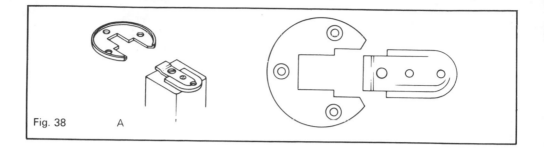

Fig. 38   A

Fig. 38 A detachable leg fitting for light tables such as coffee or occasional tables. **A**, the circular (top) plate is screwed to the underside of the top or frame while the bottom plate is screwed to the top of the leg.

Fig. 39 Lay-on hinge. This is a representative model of a range of several which require no cutting in or recessing. As their name implies, they simply lie on the surface of the door/stile and are screwed into place.

A shows the hinge applied to a lay-on door which overlaps the stile to a greater or lesser extent so that a part of the stile can be left exposed as a decorative feature. To fix, screw the end of the hinge to the door with the leading edge positioned away from the door edge by a distance equivalent to the overlap required. Then screw the end of the hinge to the stile with the leading edge of the hinge flush with the edge of the stile. Close the door and adjust the screws to achieve a perfect fit.

B illustrates the fixing for inset doors, where the door closes between stiles. To fix, screw the end of the hinge to the stile and set it in by an amount equal to the thickness of the door. The other end is then screwed to the door with its leading edge flush with the edge of the door. Again, close the door and adjust the screws.

C the hinge applied to a centre fitting. Two doors can be hinged to one central stile provided that packing is used as shown to give the necessary clearance for the doors to open simultaneously.

This type of hinge can also be obtained spring-loaded to hold the door securely in the open or closed position, eliminating the need for catches or stays.

Fig. 40 A simple magnetic catch which is 'face-fixing'; that is, planted on and screwed to the inside face of the door. The plate is, of course, fixed so that it engages with the magnet when the door is closed.

Fig. 41 The 'Tutch Latch'. This eliminates the need for knobs or handles on a door as it is secured automatically when closed while a light push on the door suffices to release the catch mechanism and allow it to open.

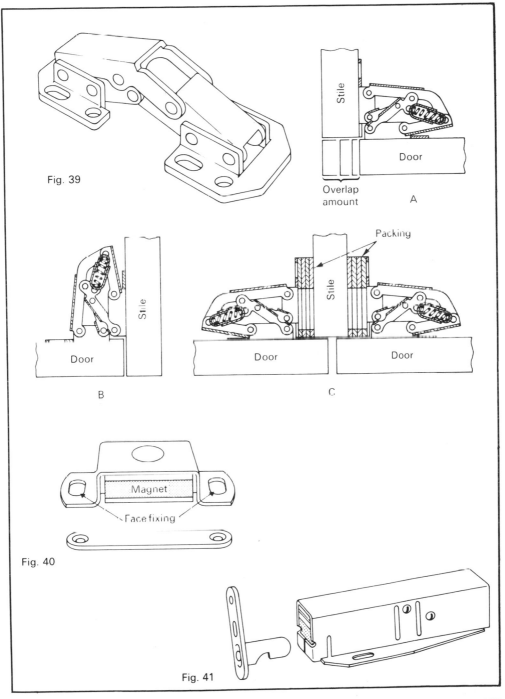

Fig. 39

Stile

Door

Overlap
amount

A

Stile

Door

B

Packing

Stile

Door

Door

C

Magnet

Face fixing

Fig. 40

Fig. 41

115

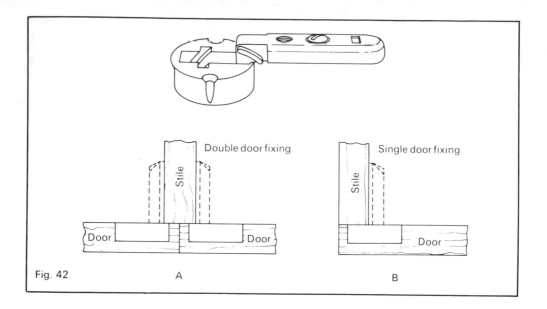

Fig. 42   Double door fixing   Single door fixing

A   B

Fig. 42 The 'Mepla' hinge. One of the several patterns of concealed hinges for use with lay-on doors, either as a single or a double fixing. Can be obtained to be knocked-in, in diagram, or with a threaded barrel to screw in.

Fig. 43 (opp. top right) Some KD fittings. **A** is a typical cam-lever locking device; **B** a slotted corner fixing plate—the heads of roundhead screws are inserted through the circular apertures and the shanks slide down the slots; **C** one of the many magnetic catches available, with its plate; **D** plastic dowel for mitred corners; **E** a 'Flushmount' fitting; **F** an ordinary wood screw and a chipboard screw side by side—note how the latter is threaded throughout its length.

Fig. 44 (opp. centre) Two typical cylindrical hinges.

Fig. 45 (opp. bottom left) Close-up of a cam-lever locking device, the cam or tongue just protruding. It is operated by means of a screwdriver inserted in the slot.

Fig. 46 (opp. bottom right) **A** corner jointing block; **B** the ever-useful dowel screw with washer and wing nut.

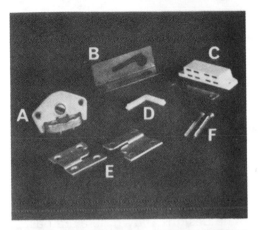

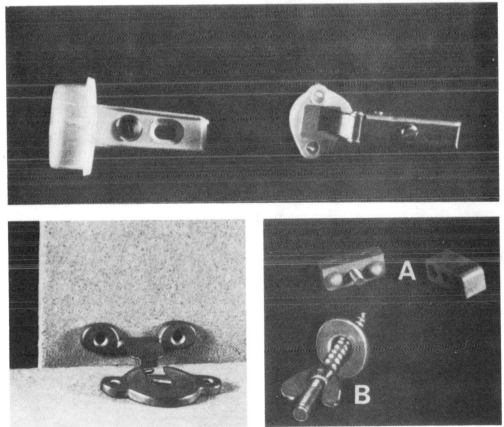

Chapter 12
Designs for Furniture

Kitchen furniture

The designs shown here are basic ones and comprise only two main units, the single cupboard and the double cupboard.

Fig. 1B shows the double cupboard which, like the single one in Fig. 1A, can be made up from chipboard. Some softwood is needed, notably for the front and back carcase rails, and also for the drawer slides.

Joints for the solid timber pediment rail can be glued and screwed to the top before the latter is fixed down. The top, ends, bottom and carcase rails can all be fixed with corner jointing blocks as shown in Chapter 11, Fig. 17, although it would be better to use a cam-lever locking device of the type shown either in Fig. 28 or 29 to fix the carcase to the ends as it exerts a considerable tightening action.

Inset doors are shown but there is no reason why lay-on doors should not be fitted as in Chapter 11, Figs. 3, 5, 6, 16, 21, 39 and 44, which all show suitable hinges. Note the simplicity of the drawer construction, and the slides employed to eliminate such things as drawer rails and kickers. The drawer is made up primarily as a tray with a hardboard bottom, the latter supported by lengths of quadrant beading, Fig. 1D. Then the softwood drawer slides are pinned and glued to the edges of the false front, and finally the true drawer front is glued and screwed to the false front.

By adopting one or other of the methods shown in Fig. 1C the shelves can be made fully adjustable for height. Six different kinds of shelf support are displayed. Nos. 1 to 4 are simply 'peg' type fittings which are a push-fit into holes bored to receive them. Although it is not strictly necessary, it is better to buy the bushes which are normally supplied with each kind and to sink each bush into a pre-bored hole. Nos. 5 and 6 are metal strip bookcase fittings, and you can see the two types of metal supporting lugs which lock into either kind of strip.

Naturally, the tops must be clad with something which will withstand hard wear, and a plastics laminate is the obvious choice; the edges will need cladding, too. The 'Tutch Latch', Chapter 11, Fig. 41, is ideal for use on

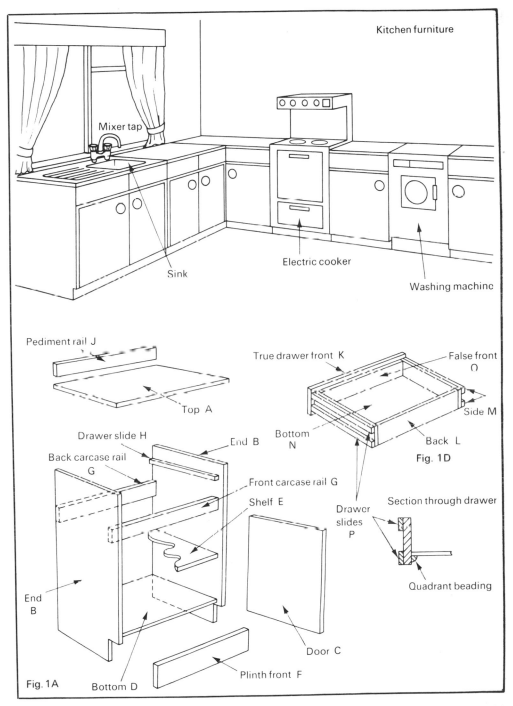

Kitchen furniture

Mixer tap

Sink

Electric cooker

Washing machine

Pediment rail J

Top A

True drawer front K

False front O

Side M

Bottom N

Back L

Fig. 1D

Drawer slide H

End B

Back carcase rail G

Front carcase rail G

Shelf E

Drawer slides P

Section through drawer

Quadrant beading

End B

Door C

Fig. 1A

Bottom D

Plinth front F

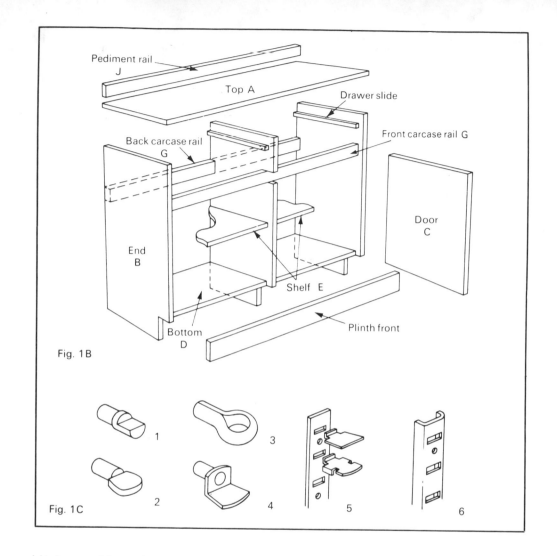

Fig. 1B

Pediment rail J

Top A

Drawer slide

Back carcase rail G

Front carcase rail G

End B

Door C

Shelf E

Bottom D

Plinth front

Fig. 1C

1

2

3

4

5

6

kitchen cabinet doors, as a door can be opened by pressing on it with the knee if the hands are full. But, it is not at all suitable where young children are about and something more positive like a strong magnetic catch could be better.

Blockboard, chipboard or plywood could be utilized for the units, but whichever you choose the edges will need treatment of some sort, and Chapter 1, Fig. 1 will give you some ideas.

N.B. Throughout: millimetres above; imperial inches in brackets.

Double Unit Parts

Part	Quantity & description	Dimensions
A	1 top	$1045 \times 530 \times 15$ ($41\frac{1}{4} \times 21 \times \frac{5}{8}$)
B	3 ends	$880 \times 530 \times 15$ ($34\frac{5}{8} \times 21 \times \frac{5}{8}$)
C	2 doors	$600 \times 500 \times 15$ ($23\frac{3}{4} \times 19\frac{3}{4} \times \frac{5}{8}$)
D	2 bottoms	$515 \times 500 \times 15$ ($20\frac{1}{4} \times 19\frac{3}{4} \times \frac{5}{8}$)
E	2 shelves	$515 \times 500 \times 15$ ($20\frac{1}{4} \times 19\frac{3}{4} \times \frac{5}{8}$)
F	1 plinth front	$1045 \times 140 \times 15$ ($41\frac{1}{4} \times 5\frac{1}{2} \times \frac{5}{8}$)
G	2 carcase rails (solid timber)	$1015 \times 65 \times 22$ ($40 \times 2\frac{1}{2} \times \frac{7}{8}$)
H	4 drawer slides (solid timber)	$515 \times 20 \times 10$ ($20\frac{1}{4} \times \frac{3}{4} \times \frac{3}{8}$)
J	1 pediment rail (solid timber)	$1045 \times 50 \times 10$ ($41\frac{1}{4} \times 2 \times \frac{3}{8}$)
K	2 drawer fronts	$515 \times 125 \times 15$ ($20\frac{1}{4} \times 5 \times \frac{5}{8}$)
L	2 drawer backs	$475 \times 110 \times 10$ ($18\frac{3}{4} \times 4\frac{3}{8} \times \frac{3}{8}$)
M	4 drawer sides	$380 \times 110 \times 10$ ($15 \times 4\frac{3}{8} \times \frac{3}{8}$)
N	2 drawer bottoms (hardboard)	$475 \times 380 \times 5$ ($18\frac{3}{4} \times 15 \times \frac{1}{4}$)
O	2 false drawer fronts	$475 \times 98 \times 15$ ($18\frac{3}{4} \times 3\frac{7}{8} \times \frac{5}{8}$)
P	8 drawer slides (solid timber)	$380 \times 45 \times 10$ ($15 \times 1\frac{3}{4} \times \frac{3}{8}$)

Single Unit Parts

Part	Quantity & description	Dimensions
A	1 top	$530 \times 530 \times 15$ ($21 \times 21 \times \frac{5}{8}$)
B	2 ends	$880 \times 530 \times 15$ ($34\frac{5}{8} \times 21 \times \frac{5}{8}$)
C	1 door	$600 \times 500 \times 15$ ($23\frac{3}{4} \times 19\frac{3}{4} \times \frac{5}{8}$)

D	1 bottom	515 × 500 × 15 ($20\frac{1}{4}$ × $19\frac{3}{4}$ × $\frac{5}{8}$)
E	1 shelf	515 × 500 × 15 ($20\frac{1}{4}$ × $19\frac{3}{4}$ × $\frac{5}{8}$)
F	1 plinth front	530 × 140 × 15 (21 × $5\frac{1}{2}$ × $\frac{5}{8}$)
G	2 carcase rails (solid timber)	500 × 65 × 22 ($19\frac{3}{4}$ × $2\frac{1}{2}$ × $\frac{7}{8}$)
H	2 drawer slides (solid timber)	515 × 20 × 10 ($20\frac{1}{4}$ × $\frac{3}{4}$ × $\frac{3}{8}$)
J	1 pediment rail (solid timber)	538 × 50 × 10 ($21\frac{1}{5}$ × 2 × $\frac{3}{8}$)
K	1 drawer front	515 × 125 × 15 ($20\frac{1}{4}$ × 5 × $\frac{5}{8}$)
L	1 drawer back	475 × 110 × 10 ($18\frac{3}{4}$ × $4\frac{3}{8}$ × $\frac{3}{8}$)
M	2 drawer sides	380 × 110 × 10 (15 × $4\frac{3}{8}$ × $\frac{3}{8}$)
N	1 drawer bottom (hardboard)	475 × 380 × 5 ($18\frac{3}{4}$ × 15 × $\frac{1}{5}$)
O	1 false drawer front	475 × 98 × 15 ($18\frac{3}{4}$ × $3\frac{7}{8}$ × $\frac{5}{8}$)
P	4 drawer slides (solid timber)	380 × 45 × 10 (15 × $1\frac{3}{4}$ × $\frac{3}{8}$)

All dimensions are nett; add about 10mm. ($\frac{3}{8}$in.) to lengths and 5mm. ($\frac{1}{5}$in.) to widths to allow for cutting and trimming. (Applies throughout this section.)

Wall cabinet with sliding doors

Deservedly popular, this type of cabinet can accommodate large quantities of crockery and utensils. It is relatively straightforward to construct, has no back and is screwed and plugged directly to the wall.

The basic parts are shown in Fig. 2A and are joined together by means of corner jointing blocks plus a woodworking adhesive (see Chapter 11, Fig. 17). In addition, the same type of blocks can be used for fixing the cabinet to the wall, being screwed to the back edges of the carcase.

All the parts are cut from 10mm. ($\frac{3}{8}$in.) board. Lengths of twin-grooved mouldings to accept the sliding doors are pinned and glued flush to the front edges of parts B, C and D, while another length is similarly fixed to the underside of C to run parallel to the moulding on D.

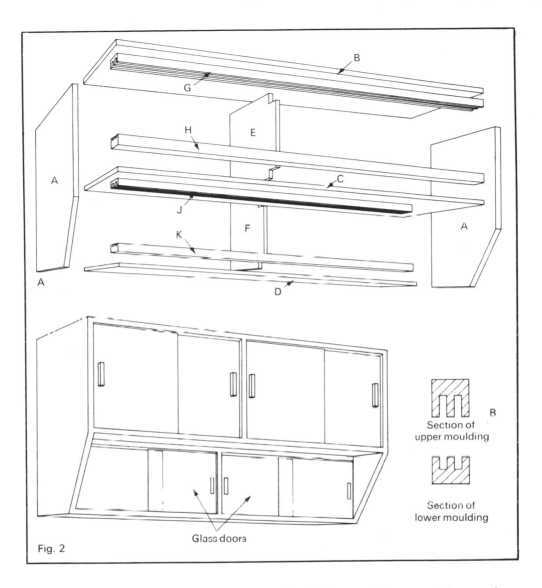

Section of
upper moulding

Section of
lower moulding

Glass doors

Fig. 2

The mouldings are stock items at any Do-It-Yourself shop, and the sections are shown in Fig. 2B. Note that the depth of the grooves in the upper moulding is twice that in the lower moulding. This enables the doors to be inserted easily by pushing them into the upper grooves first and then allowing them to drop into the lower ones. Another point to watch is that the central partitions E and F are notched out to accept the mouldings.

Blockboard, chipboard or plywood can be used for this design. If you have a painted finish—which would be very sensible for kitchen use—you will,

123

of course, have to cover the exposed edges in one of the ways shown in Chapter 1, Fig. 1.

The doors can be glass, sheets of laminated plastics or a combination of both as in the diagram. Ideally, non-glazed doors of this type should be of 2mm. ($\frac{3}{32}$in.) plywood, faced each side with a veneer or a plastics laminate to prevent 'bowing'.

Parts	Quantity & description	Dimensions
A	2 ends	760 × 300 × 10 (30 × 11$\frac{7}{8}$ × $\frac{3}{8}$)
B	1 top	1480 × 300 × 10 (58$\frac{1}{4}$ × 11$\frac{7}{8}$ × $\frac{3}{8}$)
C	1 middle shelf	1480 × 300 × 10 (58$\frac{1}{8}$ × 11$\frac{7}{8}$ × $\frac{3}{8}$)
D	1 bottom shelf	1480 × 225 × 10 (58$\frac{1}{4}$ × 8$\frac{7}{8}$ × $\frac{3}{8}$)
E	1 upper central partition	420 × 300 × 10 (16$\frac{1}{2}$ × 11$\frac{7}{8}$ × $\frac{3}{8}$)
F	1 lower central partition	310 × 300 × 10 (12$\frac{1}{4}$ × 11$\frac{7}{8}$ × $\frac{3}{8}$)
G and J	2 lengths grooved moulding, each 1480mm. (58$\frac{1}{4}$in.) long, upper section	
H and K	2 lengths grooved moulding, each 1480mm. (58$\frac{1}{4}$in.) long, upper section	

Wall unit

Although this appears to be a quite complicated design, it is really a perfectly straightforward one to build and illustrates well how modern fittings and materials can simplify what would otherwise be an intricate job. Perhaps the trickiest point is to remember that the bottom ends of the vertical panels will have to be scribed and cut to fit over any skirting board that may exist.

All main parts except the natural timber underframe rails at D can be block-board, chipboard or plywood. However, ready-veneered panels which also have their edges veneered would be ideal, the only disadvantage being that

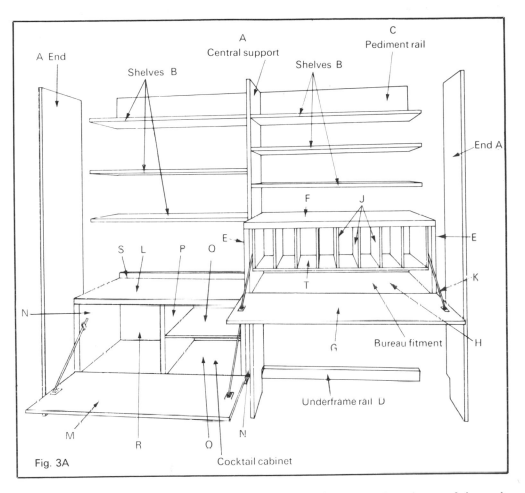

Fig. 3A

Cocktail cabinet

the measurements of your design must conform to the sizes of boards available. The backs of the cocktail cabinet and the bureau fitment, and also the pigeon holes in the bureau can be 5mm. ($\frac{3}{16}$in.) plywood.

Let us dispose of the shelves at B first. They are all adjustable and can be supported by any of the fittings shown in Fig. 1C. If you wish to fix them permanently, corner jointing blocks as in Chapter 11, Fig. 17 could be the answer, or they can be recessed into the ends, and Fig. 3B shows the several ways of doing this.

The rigidity of the framework derives from the joints between the ends A and the rails C, one end and the bureau fitment, the other end and the cocktail fitment, the fittings to the central support A, and the underframe rail D. Note that the underframe rail D is notched into the ends A and the central support, and then glued and screwed into place. It must be located

125

Not more than a third
of thickness

End

End

Notch

Shelf

Shelf

Disadvantage that joint shows

Shelf notched round so that
joint does not show

Fig. 3B

above the height of the skirting board. Screwing the rail C to the wall (inserting the screws into wall plugs, of course) will ensure a good fixing at the top, Fig. 3A.

Other joints can be made with corner jointing blocks, or the KD cam lever locking plate shown in Fig. 28, or the plastic dowels in Fig. 2, both in Chapter 11. The requirement is, of course, that whichever fixing device is used should not be readily apparent. The central partition P can be dowelled and glued in position, as can the gallery rail S.

The hinges on the fall fronts G and M could well be lengths of continuous piano hinge, and bureau stays also need to be fitted. The magnetic catches in Chapter 11, Fig. 40 would be ideal for keeping the fronts closed.

Parts	Quantity & description	Dimensions
A	2 ends and 1 centre support	$2130 \times 305 \times 22$ $(85 \times 12 \times \frac{7}{8})$
B	6 shelves	$942 \times 305 \times 22$ $(37 \times 12 \times \frac{7}{8})$
C	1 pediment rail	$1906 \times 150 \times 22$ $(75 \times 6 \times \frac{7}{8})$
D	1 underframe rail	$1950 \times 60 \times 30$ $(77\frac{3}{4} \times 2\frac{3}{8} \times 1\frac{1}{5})$
E	2 bureau ends	$380 \times 380 \times 22$ $(15 \times 15 \times \frac{7}{8})$
F	1 bureau top	$942 \times 380 \times 22$ $(37 \times 15 \times \frac{7}{8})$
G	1 fall front	$898 \times 380 \times 22$ $(35\frac{1}{4} \times 15 \times \frac{7}{8})$
H	1 bureau back (hardboard)	$898 \times 336 \times 3$ $(35\frac{1}{4} \times 13\frac{1}{4} \times \frac{1}{8})$
J	9 divisions (plywood)	$305 \times 305 \times 5$ $(12 \times 12 \times \frac{1}{5})$
K	1 bureau bottom	$898 \times 377 \times 22$ $(35\frac{1}{4} \times 14\frac{3}{4} \times \frac{7}{8})$
L	1 cabinet top	$942 \times 380 \times 22$ $(37 \times 15 \times \frac{7}{8})$
M	1 cabinet fall front	$898 \times 380 \times 22$ $(35\frac{1}{4} \times 15 \times \frac{7}{8})$
N	2 cabinet ends	$380 \times 380 \times 22$ $(15 \times 15 \times \frac{7}{8})$
O	1 cabinet bottom	$898 \times 377 \times 22$ $(35\frac{1}{4} \times 14\frac{3}{4} \times \frac{7}{8})$

P	1 cabinet division	$336 \times 305 \times 22$
		$(13\frac{1}{4} \times 12 \times \frac{7}{8})$
Q	1 cabinet shelf (plywood)	$876 \times 305 \times 5$
		$(34\frac{1}{2} \times 12 \times \frac{1}{5})$
R	1 cabinet back (hardboard)	$898 \times 336 \times 3$
		$(35\frac{1}{4} \times 13\frac{1}{4} \times \frac{1}{8})$
S	1 gallery rail	$942 \times 23 \times 12$
		$(37 \times \frac{7}{8} \times \frac{1}{2})$
T	1 bureau fitment bottom panel	$898 \times 305 \times 305$
		$(35\frac{1}{4} \times 12 \times 12)$

Sideboard

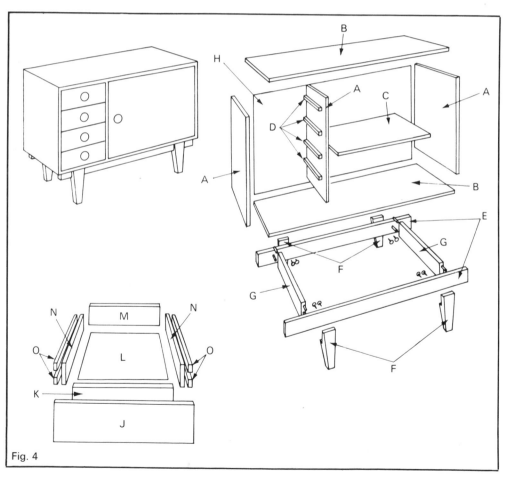

Fig. 4

The sideboard, Fig. 4, comprises a carcase constructed from man-made boards which is mounted on legs assembled in the form of a stool. It is, of course, made from solid timber, preferably hardwood. The back and the drawer bottoms are cut from hardboard.

Corner jointing blocks can be employed to assemble the carcase panels, and also to connect the stool to the underside of the carcase. On the stool, the cross rails G are dowelled to the rails E, while the latter are glued and screwed into notches cut in the top ends of the legs F. The shelf C can be supported by one or other of the several fixings shown in Fig. 1C or, if preferred, it can lie on bearers screwed and glued to the ends. The drawers are similar to those employed on the kitchen units in Fig. 1. The hardboard back is pinned and glued to the rear edges of the carcase.

Parts	Quantity & description	Dimensions
A	3 ends	$480 \times 460 \times 22$ $(18\frac{7}{8} \times 18 \times \frac{7}{8})$
B	1 top and 1 bottom	$1200 \times 460 \times 22$ $(47\frac{1}{4} \times 18 \times \frac{7}{8})$
C	1 shelf	$678 \times 460 \times 22$ $(26\frac{3}{4} \times 18 \times \frac{7}{8})$
D	8 drawer guides (solid wood)	$380 \times 22 \times 12$ $(15 \times \frac{7}{8} \times \frac{1}{2})$
E	2 long rails (solid wood)	$1100 \times 48 \times 20$ $(43\frac{1}{4} \times 1\frac{7}{8} \times \frac{3}{4})$
F	4 legs (solid wood)	$376 \times 60 \times 48$ $(14\frac{3}{4} \times 2\frac{3}{8} \times 1\frac{7}{8})$
G	2 short rails (solid wood)	$305 \times 48 \times 20$ $(12 \times 1\frac{7}{8} \times \frac{3}{4})$
H	1 back (hardboard)	$1200 \times 524 \times 3$ $(47\frac{1}{4} \times 20\frac{5}{8} \times \frac{1}{8})$
J	4 drawer fronts	$456 \times 120 \times 22$ $(18 \times 4\frac{3}{4} \times \frac{7}{8})$
K	4 false drawer fronts	$400 \times 110 \times 16$ $(15\frac{3}{4} \times 4\frac{3}{8} \times \frac{5}{8})$
L	4 drawer bottoms (hardboard)	$400 \times 362 \times 3$ $(15\frac{3}{4} \times 14\frac{1}{4} \times \frac{1}{8})$
M	4 drawer backs	$400 \times 110 \times 16$ $(15\frac{3}{4} \times 4\frac{3}{8} \times \frac{5}{8})$
N	8 drawer sides	$362 \times 110 \times 16$ $(14\frac{1}{4} \times 4\frac{3}{8} \times \frac{5}{8})$
O	16 drawer slides	$362 \times 120 \times 22$ $(14\frac{1}{4} \times 4\frac{3}{4} \times \frac{7}{8})$

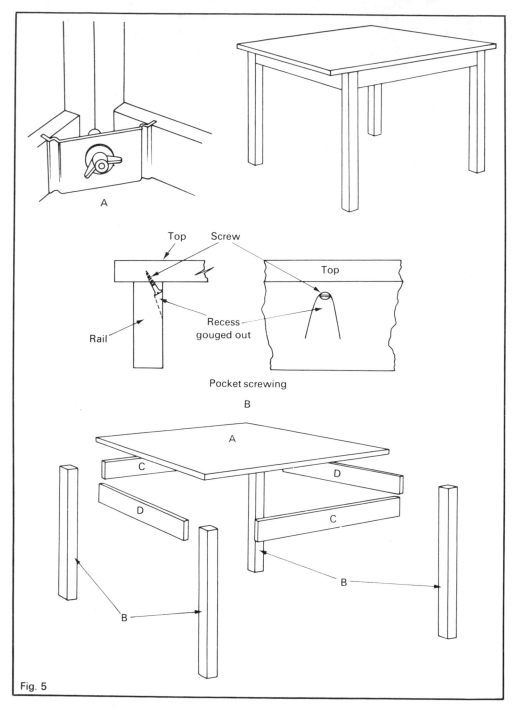

Top Screw

Rail

Recess
gouged out

Top

Pocket screwing

B

A

C

D

D

C

B

B

B

Fig. 5

Square-top table

The legs and rails of the useful table illustrated in Fig. 5 are made from natural timber, only the top being man-made board. Blockboard, chipboard or plywood are all suitable for the top, but in every case the edges will need treatment, and Chapter 1, Fig. 1 shows the various methods from which to choose.

If you use blockboard or plywood the top could be sanded down and polished, although the result will not necessarily be very exciting. If the surface turns out to be attractive, then it is purely accidental; if you want such boards faced with decorative veneers then you must order them as such or, of course, veneer them yourself.

Should you choose chipboard, then clearly it will have to be covered with something and unless you use a paint finish this leaves only veneer or a plastics laminate. All this leads to the fact that if either of these is used you should employ a solid wood edging as in Chapter 1, Fig. 1B or E. By so doing, the edge of the veneer or laminate is protected and will not be damaged or liable to be 'picked-up' by everyday wear and tear.

One of the best ways of fixing the legs to the rails is by means of the table brace plate shown in Chapter 11, Fig. 36 or 37. Pocket screwing as shown at Fig. 5B can be used for screwing down the top to the rails and, if necessary, glue blocks can be employed to strengthen the joint.

Parts	Quantity & description	Dimensions
A	1 top	990 × 685 × 25 (39 × 27 × 1)
B	4 legs	710 × 55 × 55 (28 × $2\frac{1}{6}$ × $2\frac{1}{6}$)
C	2 long rails	780 × 60 × 23 ($30\frac{3}{4}$ × $2\frac{3}{8}$ × $\frac{7}{8}$)
D	2 short rails	475 × 60 × 23 ($18\frac{3}{4}$ × $2\frac{3}{8}$ × $\frac{7}{8}$)

Dining chair

The back legs of this chair, Fig. 6, have been kept straight rather than curved to facilitate construction. However, this does mean that the seat needs to be a trifle deeper than normal and a good depth would be about 480mm.

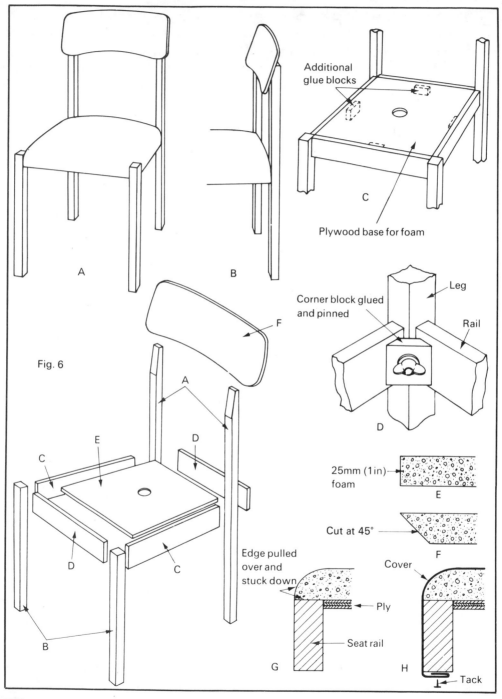

Additional glue blocks

Plywood base for foam

C

Corner block glued and pinned

Leg

Rail

D

25mm (1in) foam

E

Cut at 45°

F

Edge pulled over and stuck down

Ply

Seat rail

G

Cover

Tack

H

Fig. 6

A

B

F

A

E

C

D

D

C

B

($18\frac{7}{8}$in.). It will then accommodate the natural postural curve of the occupant.

The most important joints in any chair are the ones between the back legs and the side rails of the seat. In this design, all four corner joints are made in a way which imparts great strength and rigidity. A corner block is glued and screwed into each corner as shown at D; note that the blocks are set down 6mm. ($\frac{1}{4}$in.) from the top edges of the seat rail so that when the plywood base is inserted it can be screwed down on the blocks—this helps to reinforce the frame considerably.

Chapter 11, Fig. 25 shows the dowel screw which, with a washer and a wing nut, is used to make the joint. The woodscrew-threaded end of the dowel screw is inserted into a pre-bored hole in the leg and twisted home. Do this by running the wing-nut down to the end of the metal-threaded portion and using it to obtain leverage. Then insert the protruding end through a hole bored in the corner block and screw on the washer and wing nut, tightening the latter as hard as possible.

An extra glue block glued and screwed on at the centre of each seat rail is a good idea as each one acts as an additional support for the plywood base. By the way, a 25mm. (1in.) diameter hole bored at the centre of the plywood base will allow air to escape easily when the plastics foam seat pad is compressed.

From B you can see that the laminated back panel is slightly curved. Chapter 9, Fig. 4C shows you the set-up for doing this. The panel itself is screwed and glued to the back legs, the screws being driven in from the back.

Either plastics of latex foam can be used for the upholstered pad; you will need a piece 25mm. (1in.) thick, E, a few millimetres larger all round than the seat size. At F you can see how the edge is cut at an angle of about 45 deg. so that the edge can be pulled over and stuck down (see G) to give a neat, rounded appearance. Remember that you will need to cut out a notch at each corner to fit round the legs.

The cover is taken right over the foam and the seat rail and is tacked through a double thickness H, into the underside of the rail. It will also need to be notched out to fit round the tops of the legs, and the resulting flaps can be tacked or stuck down.

Parts	Quantity & description	Dimensions
A	2 back legs	$750 \times 35 \times 25$ ($29\frac{1}{2} \times 1\frac{3}{8} \times 1$)
B	2 front legs	$445 \times 30 \times 30$ ($17\frac{1}{2} \times 1\frac{1}{4} \times 1\frac{1}{4}$)
C	2 side seat rails	$405 \times 65 \times 22$ ($15\frac{7}{8} \times 2\frac{1}{2} \times \frac{7}{8}$)

D	2 front and back seat rails	$390 \times 65 \times 22$
		$(15\frac{3}{8} \times 2\frac{1}{2} \times \frac{7}{8})$
E	1 seat ply	$405 \times 390 \times 6$
		$(15\frac{7}{8} \times 15\frac{3}{8} \times \frac{1}{4})$
F	1 back (plywood)	$465 \times 150 \times 10$
		$(18\frac{1}{4} \times 6 \times \frac{3}{8})$
	1 piece plastics or latex foam	$480 \times 480 \times 25$
		$(18\frac{7}{8} \times 18\frac{7}{8} \times 1)$

Fireside chair

As with the design for the dining chair, the frame of this one, Fig. 7, has been kept as square as possible to simplify construction. The arms and the seat rails could be plywood, but the frame is made up in natural hardwood.

The joints are mainly conventional mortise and tenon and, because the back seat rail is fixed between the side seat rails and not between the back legs as is usual, a major weak spot has been eliminated. The arms, however, are dowelled into the back legs and on to the tops of the front legs with two dowels at each joint. As you can see, the arms are notched around the back.

Note the use of different types of springing—rubber webbing for the back, and tension springs for the seat—this kind of combination is quite normal and permissible.

Take the rubber webbing right round the rails and tack it as shown in Fig. 7B. Note how the rails are rounded off to avoid chafing the webbing, also that the length per webbing shown in the list of parts allows about 5 per cent for tensioning.

Details of fixing tension springs are given in Chapter 10, Fig. 1. When using this type of spring it is a good idea to cover the spring assembly with a piece of fabric to prevent nails, screw heads or sharp metal corners snagging the underside of the cushion cover.

Full details of the various types of cushion are given in Chapter 10, Figs. 4, 5 and 6. The minimum thicknesses for either latex foam or high density polyether foam would be 75mm. (3in.) for back cushions, and 100mm. (4in.) for seat cushions; these are the thinnest cushions which would give any degree of comfort.

Parts	Quantity & description	Dimensions
A	2 front legs	$490 \times 45 \times 45$
		$(19\frac{1}{4} \times 1\frac{3}{4} \times 1\frac{3}{4})$

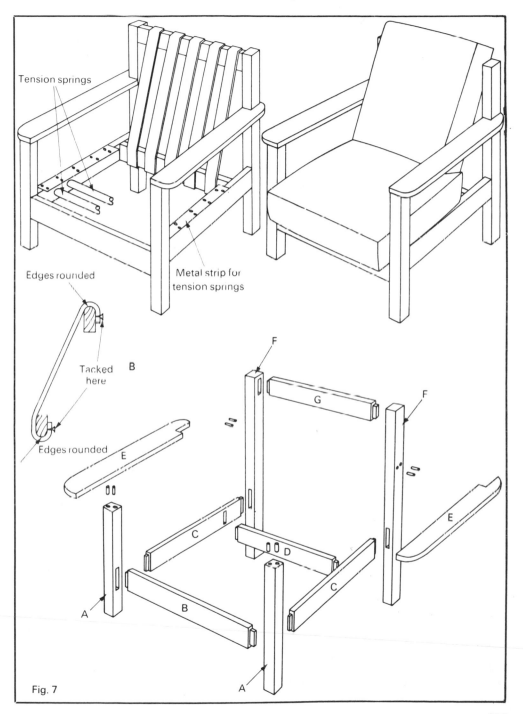

Tension springs

Edges rounded

Tacked here

B

Edges rounded

Metal strip for tension springs

E

F

G

F

C

D

C

B

A

A

E

Fig. 7

135

B	1 front seat rail	$480 \times 70 \times 23$ $(18\frac{7}{8} \times 2\frac{3}{4} \times \frac{7}{8})$
C	2 side seat rails	$520 \times 70 \times 23$ $(20\frac{1}{2} \times 2\frac{3}{4} \times \frac{7}{8})$
D	1 back seat rail	$524 \times 70 \times 23$ $(20\frac{5}{8} \times 2\frac{3}{4} \times \frac{7}{8})$
E	2 arms	$590 \times 75 \times 23$ $(23\frac{1}{4} \times 3 \times \frac{7}{8})$
F	2 back legs	$790 \times 45 \times 45$ $(31\frac{1}{8} \times 1\frac{3}{4} \times 1\frac{3}{4})$
G	1 top back rail	$480 \times 70 \times 23$ $(18\frac{7}{8} \times 2\frac{3}{4} \times \frac{7}{8})$
	5 lengths rubber webbing each	680×50 $(26\frac{3}{4} \times 2)$
	8 tension springs (seating)	435 $(17\frac{1}{8})$
	1 seat cushion	$460 \times 460 \times 100$ $(18\frac{1}{8} \times 18\frac{1}{8} \times 4)$
	1 back cushion	$460 \times 460 \times 75$ $(18\frac{1}{8} \times 18\frac{1}{8} \times 3)$

Wardrobe and dressing table fitment

The wardrobe and dressing table, Fig. 8, are further examples of large pieces of furniture rendered simple to make by the judicious use of modern fittings and large boards.

All parts except the back and drawer bottoms, which are both hardboard, and the rails and drawer stuff, which are solid timber, are from 22mm. ($\frac{7}{8}$in.) boards. Corner jointing blocks, Chapter 11, Fig. 17, can be utilized for joining the main carcase panels, namely: A to B, C to A, E to C and A; also O to P, Q to O, S to Q and O; also T to A and O. Note that the ends have to be notched out to accept the plinth front E. Fig. 8 gives details.

The front and back drawer rails X are dowelled into the ends A, with two dowels at each joint, while the drawer slides and guides are glued and screwed to the ends and the drawer sides. Pin and glue the hardboard back to the rear of the carcase.

The drawers are of similar construction to those in the kitchen units, having a false front to which the drawer sides are glued and screwed. Hardboard panels can be employed for the drawer bottoms and, as is shown in diagram Fig. 8B, they are supported by lengths of quadrant beading which are glued and pinned in position.

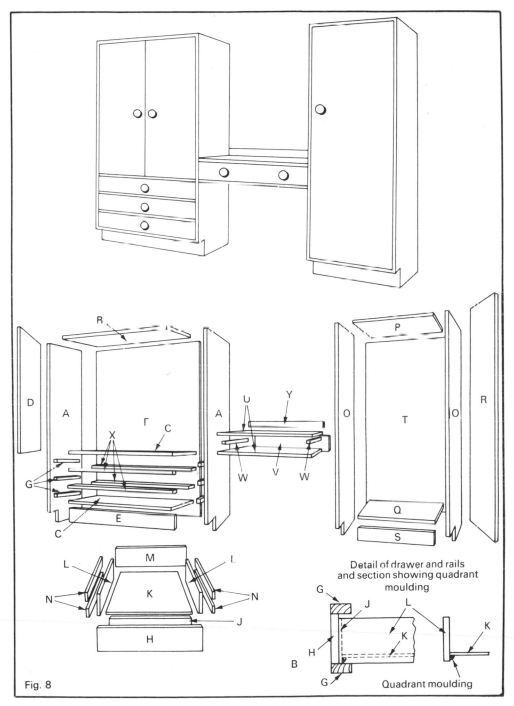

Detail of drawer and rails
and section showing quadrant
moulding

Quadrant moulding

Fig. 8

Although ordinary hinges are adequate for the doors, continuous piano hinges would look better and would give a better closing movement. To keep them closed, use a magnetic catch at the top and the bottom. Metal hanging rails (chromium plated) can be purchased, and they are supplied complete with fixing collars.

Parts	Quantity & description	Dimensions
A	2 ends	$1980 \times 530 \times 22$ $(78 \times 20\frac{7}{8} \times \frac{7}{8})$
B	1 top	$1056 \times 530 \times 22$ $(41\frac{5}{8} \times 20\frac{7}{8} \times \frac{7}{8})$
C	2 bottoms	$1056 \times 530 \times 22$ $(41\frac{5}{8} \times 20\frac{7}{8} \times \frac{7}{8})$
D	2 doors	$1440 \times 528 \times 22$ $(56\frac{3}{4} \times 20\frac{3}{4} \times \frac{7}{8})$
E	1 plinth front	$1056 \times 110 \times 22$ $(41\frac{5}{8} \times 4\frac{3}{8} \times \frac{7}{8})$
F	1 back (hardboard)	$1980 \times 1100 \times 3$ $(78 \times 43\frac{1}{4} \times \frac{1}{8})$
G	6 drawer slides (solid wood)	$486 \times 22 \times 12$ $(19\frac{1}{8} \times \frac{7}{8} \times \frac{1}{2})$
H	3 drawer fronts	$1056 \times 125 \times 22$ $(41\frac{5}{8} \times 5 \times \frac{7}{8})$
J	3 false drawer fronts	$1000 \times 110 \times 16$ $(39\frac{3}{8} \times 4\frac{3}{8} \times \frac{5}{8})$
K	3 drawer bottoms(hardboard)	$1000 \times 480 \times 3$ $(39\frac{3}{8} \times 18\frac{7}{8} \times \frac{1}{8})$
L	6 drawer sides	$496 \times 110 \times 16$ $(19\frac{1}{2} \times 4\frac{3}{8} \times \frac{5}{8})$
M	3 drawer backs	$1032 \times 110 \times 16$ $(40\frac{5}{8} \times 4\frac{3}{8} \times \frac{5}{8})$
N	12 drawer guides	$496 \times 22 \times 12$ $(19\frac{1}{2} \times \frac{7}{8} \times \frac{1}{2})$
O	2 ends	$1980 \times 530 \times 22$ $(78 \times 20\frac{7}{8} \times \frac{7}{8})$
P	1 top	$530 \times 516 \times 22$ $(20\frac{7}{8} \times 20\frac{3}{8} \times \frac{7}{8})$
Q	1 bottom	$530 \times 516 \times 22$ $(20\frac{7}{8} \times 20\frac{3}{8} \times \frac{7}{8})$
R	1 door	$1826 \times 516 \times 22$ $(72 \times 20\frac{3}{8} \times \frac{7}{8})$

S	1 plinth front	$516 \times 110 \times 22$
		$(20\frac{3}{8} \times 4\frac{3}{8} \times \frac{7}{8})$
T	1 back (hardboard)	$1980 \times 560 \times 3$
		$(78 \times 22\frac{1}{4} \times \frac{1}{8})$
U	2 tops	$800 \times 530 \times 22$
		$(31\frac{1}{2} \times 20\frac{7}{8} \times \frac{7}{8})$
V	1 back (hardboard)	$800 \times 169 \times 3$
		$(31\frac{1}{2} \times 6\frac{5}{8} \times \frac{1}{8})$
W	2 drawer slides (solid wood)	$486 \times 22 \times 12$
		$(19\frac{1}{8} \times \frac{7}{8} \times \frac{1}{2})$
X	4 drawer rails (solid wood)	$1056 \times 48 \times 22$
		$41\frac{5}{8} \times 1\frac{7}{8} \times \frac{7}{8})$
Y	1 pediment rail	$800 \times 38 \times 12$
		$(31\frac{1}{2} \times 1\frac{1}{2} \times \frac{1}{2})$

Single bed with headboard

The bed, Fig. 9, is a useful design which would be eminently suitable for a teenager or in the guest room.

Although suggested sizes are given in the list of parts, it is really a case of buying the mattress first and then building the bed to fit it. Besides, many readers will doubtless have spare mattresses which they will wish to use.

Obviously, the first consideration is strength, not only because of the weight of the occupant, but also because the frame has to resist the tension imposed by the rubber webbing. So, hardwood is the first choice as timber, although sound, straight grained softwood is a good runner-up.

The corners of the frame can be jointed in any one of several ways. Probably the easiest would be a simple glued and screwed butt joint with a corner block glued in; another way would be to use two sets of corner jointing blocks per joint; yet a third method would be to use a cam jointing device at each corner, although this would need reinforcing by screwing through the side rails, A, into the end rails, B. Fig. 9A shows details.

Fixing the legs is simple as they are merely glued and screwed to the side rails, A. Similarly, the cross struts C are glued to the underside of the frame and screwed up from underneath.

The shape of the headboard will be to your choice; remember that if you have a curved shape such as the one shown, you will need to edge it with one of the flexible veneer edgings. The struts F are glued and screwed to the back of the headboard; note how a slot is cut in each one so that a coach bolt, plus washer and wing-nut, can be arranged as in Fig. 9C to hold the headboard in place, and to allow it to be removed at will.

Fig. 9B illustrates the two ways of fastening the rubber webbing, both of which have been dealt with in Chapter 10.

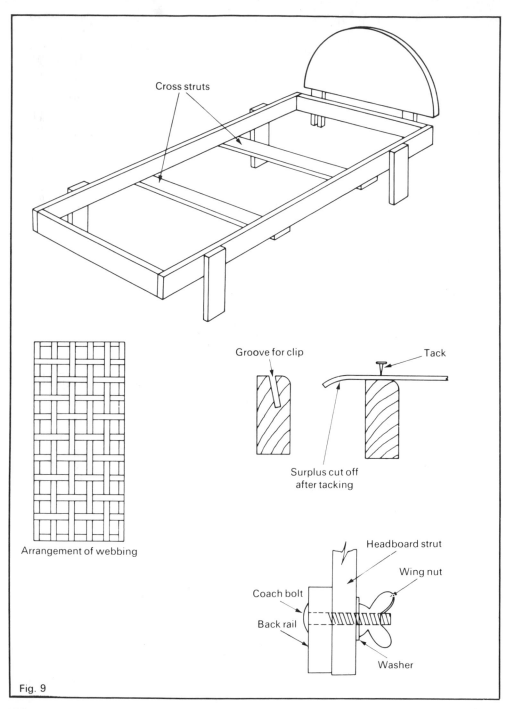

Cross struts

Groove for clip

Tack

Surplus cut off
after tacking

Arrangement of webbing

Headboard strut

Wing nut

Coach bolt

Back rail

Washer

Fig. 9

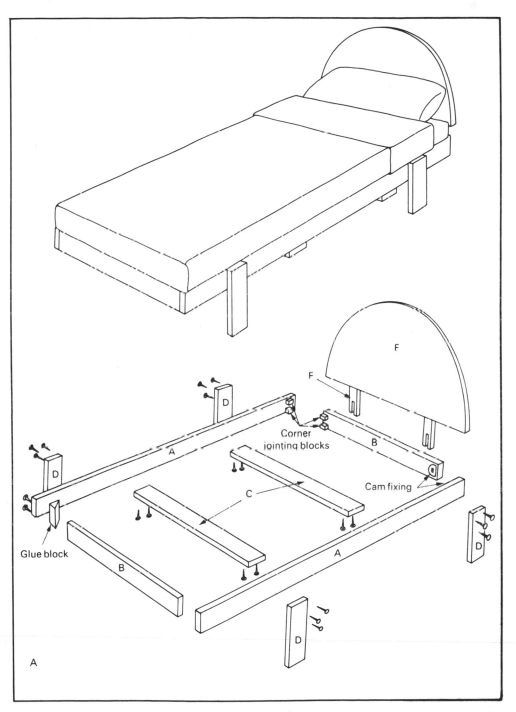

Corner jointing blocks

Cam fixing

Glue block

A

B

C

D

F

Parts	Quantity & description	Dimensions
A	2 side rails	$1980 \times 73 \times 47$ $(78 \times 2\frac{7}{8} \times 1\frac{7}{8})$
B	2 head and foot rails	$673 \times 73 \times 47$ $(26\frac{1}{2} \times 2\frac{7}{8} \times 1\frac{7}{8})$
C	2 cross struts	$762 \times 73 \times 47$ $(30 \times 2\frac{7}{8} \times 1\frac{7}{8})$
D	4 legs	$255 \times 95 \times 30$ $(10 \times 3\frac{3}{4} \times 1\frac{1}{5})$
E	1 headboard	$762 \times 380 \times 16$ $(30 \times 15 \times \frac{5}{8})$
F	2 headboard struts	$380 \times 48 \times 23$ $(15 \times 1\frac{7}{8} \times \frac{7}{8})$
	4 lengths rubber webbing each	1780×50 (70×2)
	10 lengths rubber webbing each	660×50 (26×2)

Index

143